# Praise for *Play Ni*

"For all the talk about the #MeToo and Time's Up movements, there is still little practical information available to help a woman beat back sexual harassment—until now. *Play Nice* is chock full of smart, strategic advice to help anyone suffering from toxic behavior in the workplace."

—Skip Hollandsworth,
Executive Editor, *Texas Monthly*

"For real change to occur, it is imperative that we all start holding ourselves responsible for ensuring everyone is treated respectfully. *Play Nice* is a giant step in the right direction. This book should be mandatory reading for all organizations and parents!"

—Vanessa Fox, Corp. VP,
Chief Development Officer, Jack in the Box

"It is a go-to account of legal changes as well as watershed moments that open our eyes to the ubiquitous nature of sexual harassment. A must-read for women of all ages, recognizing that although we have come a long way, we have not come far enough!"

—Jan Edgar Langbein, CEO,
Genesis Women's Shelter & Support

"This is a must-read for any human resources executive, any woman embarking on her professional career, and any bystander (male or female) who is not sure what to do when faced with bad behavior."

—Joel L. Ross, Former General
Counsel of Trammell Crow Company and
Retired Partner of Vinson & Elkins LLP

"Brigitte Kimichik and JR Tomlinson have written a critical book full of practical tips on creating workplaces that are inclusive and respectful of women. *Play Nice* is an instrument of change."

—Sharon Orlopp, CHRO,
Core Scientific, a Tech Start-Up, and Retired
Global Chief Diversity Officer at Walmart

"I am proud to have worked with an organization that has an unwavering commitment to integrity in all business operations. Part of this commitment is ensuring everyone has a safe, healthy, and respectful working environment. *Play Nice* is a spot-on guide to understanding and implementing this vitally important part of our corporate culture."

—William Geiler, Executive Vice President
of Development, Hotel & Lodging Firm

"*Play Nice* is a lively and highly practical guide to optimizing the relationships between women and men in the workplace, as well as an indispensable tool for avoiding missteps and misunderstandings. The authors are entering the conversation at exactly the right moment."

—Jonathan Kirsch, Attorney, Best-Selling Author,
and National Book Critics Circle Member

"*Play Nice is* a timely 'must-read' that provides a unique approach for responding to sexual harassment. This book is definitely a conversation starter!"

—Suzy Bashore, CIO, PGIM Real Estate Finance

# PLAY NICE

# THE SANDBOX SERIES

# PLAY NICE

## Playground Rules for Respect in the Workplace

## BRIGITTE GAWENDA KIMICHIK, JD
## JR TOMLINSON

BROWN BOOKS
PUBLISHING GROUP

*Play Nice*
*Playground Rules for Respect in the Workplace*

Brown Books Publishing Group
16250 Knoll Trail Drive, Suite 205
Dallas, Texas 75248
www.BrownBooks.com
(972) 381-0009

A New Era in Publishing®

Names: Kimichik, Brigitte Gawenda, author. | Tomlinson, J. R., author.
Title: Play nice : playground rules for respect in the workplace / Brigitte Gawenda Kimichik, JD [and] JR Tomlinson.
Description: Dallas, Texas : Brown Books Publishing Group, [2019] | Series: The sandbox series
Identifiers: ISBN 9781612542904
Subjects: LCSH: Sexual harassment--Prevention. | Respect for persons. | Personnel management.
Classification: LCC HF5549.5.S45 K56 2019 | DDC 658.3145--dc23

ISBN 978-1-61254-290-4
LCCN 2018961303

Printed in the United States
10 9 8 7 6 5 4 3 2 1

For more information or to contact the author,
please go to www.TheSandboxSeries.com.

*This book is dedicated to the men who support and respect women and the moms who raised them—and to our young family members Samantha, Nicole, and Kristina. We hope this book will continue to empower you to stand up for yourselves as you grow to be strong and independent women.*

# Contents

Authors' Note      xiii

Introduction      1

—   My Story      4
—   JR's Story      9
—   A Sobering Reality Check Regarding Women's Right to Equality      13
—   Supporting Feminism Is Not a Negative: The True Meaning      17

Chapter 1
Welcome to the Sandbox      19

—   The Meaning of the Sandbox on the Playground of the Work Environment      19
—   Company Policies and Current Legislation Are Not Sufficient      20
—   The Importance of Self-Help and the Rules of the Playground      31

Chapter 2
Where Does Bad Behavior Start,
and Where Should We Begin to Effect Change?      33

—   Education at Home, Middle School, and High School      33
—   Education in Preparation for College or University      38
—   Education in Preparation for the Workplace      43
—   What If Your Workplace Is the Entertainment Industry?      44

Chapter 3
What to Do If You're Being Harassed in the Workplace      53

—   Start with Plan A      54
—   When Implementing Plan A, Be Aware of Different Personality Types      55
    ›   Tyrant Ivan      55
    ›   Insecure Trip      55
    ›   Ego Joe      55

  — Plan A: Steps of Communication      56

  — Plan B: Filing a Formal Complaint      60

## Chapter 4
## Why Women Are Afraid to Report Sexual Harassment    73

  — Sexual Harassment Laws Are Complicated      73

  — Fear of Shame, Humiliation, and Intimidation      74

  — Fear of Retaliation      76

## Chapter 5
## Introduction of the Playground
## Rules to Help Implement Plan A    79

  — The Playground Rules and Sexual Harassment      79

  — Using the Playground Rules as Prompts      80

  — Putting Playground Rules to the Test:      81
     Real-World Examples to Illustrate How to Respond

## Chapter 6
## Our Call to Companies:
## Promoting a Workplace Cultural Change    101

  — Taking Action Adds Value to Companies and Improves the Bottom Line      103

  — Collaboration of Men and Women Can Increase Profitability      106

  — Unintended Consequences of the #MeToo Movement: Don't Make Excuses      109

  — Consider the Following Immediate Action Items      110

  — Other Playground Rules Applicable to Companies      117
     and Important for Company Employees

## Chapter 7
## Our Call to Men: We Need Your Help to Effect Change    123

  — The Importance of Male Support      123

  — Engaging Men in Discussion      125

  — Common Motivations for Sexual Harassment      127

  — Treat Others How You Want to Be Treated: The Golden Rule      129

  — An Important Historical Review      131

  — Pillar Suggestions on How Men Can Help      138

     ›   Don't Be A Bystander. Take Action to Correct Bad Behavior      138

     ›   Be a Fierce Ally of Women      139

| | | |
|---|---|---|
| › | Don't Be Afraid to Talk about Sexual Harassment with Your Colleagues, Friends, or Family Members | 140 |
| › | Ask Women for Guidance on How You Can Help | 140 |
| › | Take a Look at Your Own Training in Sexual Harassment | 141 |
| — | Examples of Behavior That Is Not Acceptable: What Constitutes Crossing the Line? | 142 |
| › | If You Wouldn't Do It to a Man | 142 |
| › | Revisiting the Playground Rules: What Is Bad Behavior? | 145 |
| › | Understand Her Body Language | 151 |
| › | Understand the Statistics—They Don't Lie | 156 |
| › | Women's Clothing and Sexual Harassment | 156 |
| › | Why Are Women—Even Today—Rarely in Positions of Power? | 158 |

## Chapter 8
## Responding to Bad Behavior
161

| | | |
|---|---|---|
| — | Cleaning Up the Language: Have We Lost Our Ability to be Civil, Polite, and Professional? | 161 |
| — | Learning to Take Control Immediately and Modify Behavior | 169 |
| — | Using the Boys' Club to Your Advantage | 175 |
| — | Don't Be a Bystander | 179 |

## Chapter 9
## As a Society, What Positive Changes Can We Implement?
183

| | | |
|---|---|---|
| — | Changes in Law | 183 |
| › | Nondisclosure Agreements | 183 |
| › | Forced Arbitration Provisions | 183 |
| › | Statute of Limitations | 184 |
| › | Require Company Reporting | 184 |
| › | Lawsuits under Title VII of the Civil Rights Act of 1964 | 185 |
| › | Title VII and the Fifteen-Employee Requirement | 185 |
| › | Legislate a 30 Percent Quota | 185 |
| › | New Tax Cuts and Jobs Act | 185 |
| — | Nonlegal Actions | 186 |
| › | Making Controversial Contract Provisions Optional | 186 |
| › | Publishing Company Efforts to Set an Example | 186 |
| › | Rally the Troops | 186 |
| › | Social Media and Campaigns | 187 |
| » | #MuteRKelly Movement | 187 |

» Time's Up Campaign 187

› Discourage Vulgarity in Language 187

› Do Not Support Harassers 188

› Teach Consent Early 188

## Chapter 10
## Takeaways for Women in the Sandbox

Takeaways for Women in the Sandbox 189

— Don't Be One of the Boys 189

— Pick Your Battles 189

— Draw a Hard Line 190

— Don't Be Afraid to Share Your Opinion 191

— Don't Be Your Assistant 191

— Don't Give Anyone a Reason to Challenge Your Abilities; Be Prepared 191

— Don't Date a Colleague 192

— Dress Professionally; Don't Be A Distraction 193

— Be Confident, but Don't Be a Bitch 193

— Monitor Your Emotions 193

— Who Are Your Allies? 194

## Conclusion
## Acknowledgments
## Notes
## About the Authors

Conclusion 195

Acknowledgments 199

Notes 201

About the Authors 225

# Authors' Note

The information and advice presented in this book regarding sexual harassment and discrimination are limited in scope and general in nature and do not take into account developments that may have taken place after the book's composition or publication. This book is not intended to provide legal, psychological, or other professional services to the reader and does not take the place of a consultation with an appropriate professional. The authors and the publisher strongly encourage the reader to consult with an appropriate professional to deal with specific issues and problems. The highly publicized cases that are discussed in this book are subject to further developments, and the reader is cautioned to ascertain the current status of all laws and legal cases mentioned here. In this book, whenever an individual is identified by first name only or by a phrase such as "Tyrant Ivan" or "Ego Joe," the name is fictional and should not be associated with any real person. Both of the authors have worked at several firms during their careers, but none of these firms are identified by name in the anecdotes included within this book. All opinions are those of the authors and do not reflect the opinions of their former firms or colleagues.

# Introduction

The statistics concerning sexual harassment are troubling. According to recent surveys, one in three women in the workforce has experienced sexual harassment, and many women do not report the abuse because they fear retaliation, fear losing their job or opportunities within the company, or are too embarrassed or ashamed.[1]

My coauthor, JR Tomlinson, and I first met in 2002 at a women's luncheon. At the time, I was a commercial real-estate and finance law partner at a midsized law firm in Dallas, Texas, and JR was a commercial real-estate broker with a local company in Dallas. Both our industries are heavily male dominated, and throughout the many years we have known each other, we have scoffed at and cried over appalling and often shocking experiences of sexual harassment, abuse, and gender discrimination and the troubling frequency of such occurrences. What we both discovered in our discussions with colleagues, other professionals, friends, and family, including many younger members of our respective fields, is a sobering reality. Despite over thirty years passing since JR and I started our careers, there has been little improvement in the toxic masculinity of the workplace culture, and company policies against sexual harassment and procedures for filing complaints have made little difference. Sexual harassment is alive and well, and the frequency is appalling. Even worse, recent news stories show us that filing a complaint with the human resources department (which we will call "HR")—assuming you have access to an HR department—will not necessarily save your job. The potential for retaliation, including abuse from supporters of the violator, further humiliation and embarrassment, bullying, and losing one's job, can be dire.

What is striking is that even in today's environment of the #MeToo movement, in which disclosure is supposedly encouraged, we have found that young women who recently entered the workforce are afraid to speak about their sexual harassment experiences publicly for fear of retaliation and loss of job promotion opportunities—even if their names and employers are not identified. Under what circumstances would that ever be acceptable? It is heartbreaking.

JR and I agreed that, one day, we would publish our collective advice on how to handle and modify the behavior of abusers, with the goal of helping a victim protect and preserve what she has worked so hard to obtain and what is rightfully hers: her job, her career, and her reputation. This also applies to victims who are men. Anyone who knows JR and I understands this subject has always been dear to our hearts. Our own experiences in very male-dominated work environments shaped who we are today and have given us more to talk about than we could ever imagine.

Of course, we agree with the Time's Up movement—there should be radical changes to stop sexual harassment once and for all. However, in reality, the changes we crave today will not occur overnight. It will take time for businesses to improve and properly enforce their human resource departments' sexual harassment policies and procedures to encourage victims to file complaints without fear of retaliation, humiliation, or loss of job. It will take several years to implement new and more effective legislation with noteworthy consequences to deter violations, and it will take many more years before there are female populations in executive-level positions of the workforce in significant enough numbers to change the sexist male-dominated culture and accompanying bad behavior. Until all of these benchmarks have been achieved, we must be realistic. Our laws and company policies have not come far enough, and we simply cannot rely on the current status to protect victims from sexual harassment and the dire consequences that can follow filing a complaint with HR. Victims first must learn how to deal with sexual harassment on their own—especially if harassment is a frequent occurrence, they do not have access to an HR department, or they do not believe their HR department handles such complaints properly or effectively. JR and I have firsthand experience.

We have several goals for this book. First: to arm victims and bystanders with basic and simple tools to help them deal with sexual harassment and violators in the work environment the very moment such behavior occurs, helping to stop such behavior in its tracks. Second: to provide examples of violative behavior and optional responses for victims and bystanders. And third: to offer companies and their leadership suggestions about how to handle victims and violators, with the goal of improving working relations between men and women in the close quarters of the working environment and improving company culture to create a more prosperous and successful company. For the purposes of this book, we call the close quarters the *Sandbox* and the working environment of the company the *Playground*. We do not take these terms lightly. We use these terms to help communicate bad behavior with basic "playground rules," which we will introduce later in this book. JR and I believe it's up to victims themselves and the women and men in leadership at companies to defend against, redirect, and modify toxic and abusive interactions and behaviors immediately when they occur.

Our advice and suggestions in this book rely on our own personal experiences throughout our respective careers and our views on events in the news when we were writing this book rather than scientific research and studies. Please take them with a grain of salt and in no way consider them legal or psychological advice. It is never a bad idea to seek professional legal or psychological services if you have any questions or concerns about your specific situation. Please also note that the primary focus of this book is on behaviors that constitute sexual harassment, such as unwelcome sexual advances, requests for sexual favors, and other verbal or physical harassment of a sexual nature (including offensive remarks about a person's gender).[2] For purposes of this book, we will call such behavior "bad behavior." This book does not intend to address behaviors involving physical violence, assault, battery, or rape, which are criminal offenses and should be reported to the local police authorities.

We hope, however, that our approach to dealing with abusers first through example scenarios, guiding rules to assist communications, suggested responses for bystanders, proposed actions to be taken by employers, and behavior dos and don'ts will be helpful in combatting sexual harassment in the work environment.

Whether you're just starting your first job, are an employee or an executive in a leadership position, or are a colleague, customer, family member, or friend, this book is for you. This book is our effort to help victims take immediate action to defend against sexual harassment using the rules many of us first learned as children on the playground— rules JR and I successfully applied throughout our careers to combat sexual harassment by learning how to "play nice" in the working environment of the company (the Sandbox).

## My Story

Imagine you are almost out of school—finally! It's time to get serious and find that first dream job. For most, that first position is a reflection of years of accomplishments in high school, college, and maybe even graduate school. You do your research, invest in new clothes, go to interviews, and then, if all goes well, you receive one or more offers. Super exciting, right? It should be!

For any male readers, now imagine you are a woman. Welcome to our playground.

I still remember some of my interviews and follow-up callbacks as if they were yesterday. Many were in-office interviews, dinners, and late-night cocktails and parties with prospective law firms who were interested in me. That was more than thirty years ago—1985. At the time, the market for good legal industry jobs was tough and highly competitive due to the financial crisis involving the savings and loan industry. After every meeting or late night with a group, I would call my parents with a report. They would ask me, "Do you think you will get a permanent offer? What do you like about the potential employer? What do you think made an impression on them or on you?" I didn't always have the answers, but I could tell they were as anxious as I was. They were so proud whenever I was invited for a callback interview with a big law firm or for a more intimate company dinner or cocktail party.

I remember one callback in particular after an interview hosted at my law school with a Houston law firm. Along with some other candidates, I was invited to the firm's cocktail party at a restaurant in Dallas. At the time, I was a second-year law student at Southern Methodist University Law School in Dallas, looking for a full-time job in the litigation section of a law firm. Accordingly, I spent the majority of the evening meeting the firm's trial attorneys. There was only one other woman in the litigation group, a senior associate with five years of practice under her belt. She ensured I met everyone in attendance, including the partners, and the evening was going well. Getting an offer would mean that I'd be working for one of the most reputable firms in Texas. Toward the end of the evening, I found myself standing momentarily alone at the bar with one of the more senior partners. He was very complimentary of me and my background. He leaned toward me and asked if we could continue the conversation up in his hotel room. "I need to make a quick call first, and then we can spend the rest of the evening discussing your potential future as an associate at the firm."

Wow. I was stunned. Did he really just ask me that? My mind raced. Go with him, and I might get an offer—but at what personal risk? What were his intentions? If I didn't go with him, what would that mean? Would he respect me for declining? If I accepted the invitation and got an offer, what would our relationship be like going forward? How would this impact my career?

He put his hand on mine to force a response. I had to decide. As calmly as I could, I smiled and said, "Thank you for the invite, but I need to get home to prepare for a new day of class work." He smiled, said it was nice to meet me, and turned back to survey the room, presumably for another "up-and-coming female associate."

I was shaken and went home to a sleepless night. I had prepared for hours for my first interview with this firm and was excited, even relieved, when I received the cocktail party invite. I'd thought it meant I was on the short list for a permanent offer, one I had been working so hard to earn, but now I feared maybe I was only a potential conquest for a firm partner totally ignorant of my actual qualifications.

I kept wondering: Would this partner have asked a male candidate to come up to his room to discuss his future? I sincerely doubted it and was very unsettled by the whole affair. It caused me to reevaluate how I had to act around—and especially present myself to—male interviewers or workplace superiors to avoid giving "the wrong impression." I thought my dress had been very conservative. Dark blue, with no cleavage, and below my knees in length. My makeup was plain, and my shoes were low in height, closed toed, and dark colored. Typical conservative wear for bank employees. I was not flirtatious in any of my communications. Was it the fact that I was female? Maybe attractive, in his view?

I left the restaurant without sharing my experience with any of the firm's attorneys or recruiting coordinators. I needed time to process what had happened to be sure my perception of the partner's inappropriate behavior was accurate. Of course, I couldn't tell my parents. My dad, a retired colonel in the German air force, would have flown to Houston to give that partner a piece of his mind!

A few weeks later, I received an offer from that firm. I respectfully declined, but not before calling the hiring partner. Letting him know what had happened was a difficult decision, but after many discussions with my closest friends and a female mentor, I made the call. He thanked me for my honesty and understood my concern that if I accepted, the incident might affect my future career at the firm. He did not, however, offer an apology or any alternative explanation for the other partner's behavior. Maybe he wasn't sure what to say, or maybe it had happened before?

Even though I spoke up about what happened, that experience haunted me. I couldn't believe a partner would violate a candidate's trust so openly without any consequence. Of course, I was naive to think that incident would be my only brush with such behavior. Many more followed, even before I fully entered the workforce. Just a few weeks later, I attended a dinner thrown by another law firm to celebrate new employment offers to candidates. One of the partners who'd previously interviewed me insisted I sit next to him, and for the rest of dinner, he made it obvious he was interested in an intimate relationship. His leg brushed up against mine; he put his arm around me; he touched my back several times and leaned in repeatedly so as not to be heard at other tables. He said I would be "an exciting addition" to his team and we could even travel together. He would be a great teacher for me and give guidance to navigating the firm.

With every pour of the wine, he became more aggressive. It was clear he was getting drunk, apparently unconcerned about repercussions. I was very uncomfortable and kept looking around the room for help. He was obvious in his flirtation, and no one seemed to care—not even the firm's recruiting staff, who were tasked with ensuring everyone in attendance enjoyed the event. I didn't want to offend him, given his state of mind, or make a scene, but then he put his hand on my knee and started moving it up my leg. I gently moved his hand back and excused myself to go to the restroom. When I returned, I conversed with others at the table and even suggested I move around the room to meet some of the other firm members. Nothing worked; he was not going to leave me alone. Accepting the firm's offer would no longer be an option. Ultimately, they lost a good candidate, and I gave up what otherwise could have been a great opportunity. That said, I later found out his colleagues had been aware of his behavior for years, and even though he was eventually asked to leave, it was only after multiple sexual harassment settlements had cost the firm dearly.

After these experiences, I became more focused on possible innuendos and comments of a sexual nature in my interactions with men. From then on, gender issues in the workplace became a personal passion, and I was consistently surprised by how often I witnessed and experienced inappropriate behavior, my first job as an attorney being no exception.

At my original law firm in Houston, Texas, I accepted a position in the trial section, where I would be trained to handle commercial business disputes in court at the local and state levels. When I arrived at the firm, however, the only woman in a different section, the commercial real-estate and finance section, had just left the firm, and her clients were demanding she be replaced by a woman. The firm wanted her replacement to be tough—a "guy's gal" who could handle men—and they thought I might be a good fit. I was asked to give the section a try for six months, and if I hated it, they would move me to litigation, as we had originally agreed. I had no idea what to expect when I accepted the challenge—but I soon learned that I would need thick skin, patience, and a much louder voice to survive and succeed. I decided to give up the trial section of the firm and to continue my career in the commercial real-estate and finance area—a field dominated by men—and I was exposed to frequent male banter and sexual harassment. I realized complaining about the behavior would not necessarily help me, especially if the violator was a partner or a valuable client to the firm, and given the frequency of the sexual harassment, it would not be realistic for me to run to HR every single time. I had to make a few decisions. I genuinely enjoyed the company of my male colleagues and working with them, and it was important that I foster good relationships. I decided that if I taught them how to treat me with respect while we worked together—showing them rather than telling—I might be more successful warding off sexual harassment. I also decided I wanted to learn how to address inappropriate behavior with proper communication as soon as it occurred to immediately put a stop to possible repetition. To help me with this endeavor, I solicited advice from my more senior colleagues, men and women, and learned how to draw delicate lines and command respect during the early stage of my career. My male colleagues accepted my instruction and became my supporters and allies. It took years of learning experiences and good mentors, male and female, to help me work through the labyrinth of possible inappropriate behaviors and to effectively combat sexual harassment. It did not take too long for me to begin mentoring our female associates accordingly.

My experiences, both positive and negative, turned me into a measured, patient, determined, and (most importantly to me) confident woman. I became a more efficient and competent attorney, a determined mother, and a stronger mentor for career advancement and for dealing with sexual harassment.

## JR's Story

JR, the coauthor of this book, endured similar experiences. After graduating college with a BBA in finance/investments, she started her career in the stocks and bonds area and likewise discovered that she was not taken as seriously as her male counterparts. Fellow male graduates who'd cheated off of her in corporate finance classes and barely pulled a C were offered positions with the training programs of large financial institutions. Meanwhile, in JR's interviews, she was asked if she could type. At her first postgraduate job in marketing for the tax shelter and limited partnership division of a real-estate investment company, JR was given menial typing tasks for executives and received less pay despite having the same title as her male counterparts. JR was not deterred. She stayed focused and took advantage of positive opportunities to pass her Series 7 and 63 licenses (exams required to trade stocks and bonds) well before her male peers.

To further her career, she interviewed and accepted a position with a large brokerage house as a financial consultant (stockbroker). The company sent her to a monthlong training in Princeton, New Jersey, with 150 other financial consultant trainees. She was one of only three women; JR was twenty-six years old, and the other two were in their midforties. After JR returned to work, she discovered the new male office manager was not welcoming of women. In fact, he had never hired a woman in the eight years he'd managed his previous office. In his words, women did not belong in a man's world (the business world) and did not make good stockbrokers. JR, meanwhile, was already managing her own million-dollar book of business and proving unequivocally otherwise. It did not matter that his company had spent thousands of dollars training JR, or that she had already generated a remarkable book of business, or that she complemented his style of obtaining clients rather than challenged it. In his mind—as he never hesitated to tell her—she would be much better suited as a buyer for a top retailer because "she was attractive and had great taste in clothes."

At the time, the few women working for her employer were equally unsupportive. JR was perceived as a threat and was told by the sole top woman producer in the office that she would have to make her own way at the company with no leads for business from her. She'd worked hard to get to the top, and JR would have to do the same. JR found out that this woman had no issue handing out leads to JR's male counterparts, however.

JR eventually felt that she had no choice but to leave the company to advance in her career, but she did not give up. She knew that she could outperform her male counterparts. JR was interested in working on large, challenging real-estate and development transactions. She knew she would have to prove herself by showing she could attract, negotiate, and successfully close these types of transactions. She could not be sure a male counterpart would give her work without getting all the credit, purposefully on his part or not. So she built her reputation as a commercial and industrial real-estate broker one carefully negotiated deal at a time on her way toward earning her colleagues' respect.

At the beginning of her career at a local real-estate broker firm in Dallas, JR was one of only a few female commercial real-estate brokers in her industry. In those days, a woman in her field had to dress, act, and speak like a man. If you were attractive, you likely would not be taken seriously. JR was strong and attractive, and if you knew JR, you knew it was not a good idea to mess with her. She learned how to play with the boys. In the mid-'80s, most brokers were independent contractors, and HR departments were a rarity in the commercial real-estate brokerage industry.

One of JR's storied tales from early in her career recounts entering the office of a fellow broker with a few of her colleagues to discuss a client project. Out of the blue, one of the brokers quietly grabbed JR's behind in the middle of the group's conversation—presumably to see her reaction or maybe to be funny. Without hesitation, she quickly reached around and grabbed the front of his pants hard with her long nails, making him jump back in surprise. "I guess you didn't like that, did you?" JR asked him under her breath. "Maybe you'll remember that when you think about grabbing my ass next time!" She did this laughingly, with humor, but he got the message. He never tried that again.

Note that she didn't yell at him or put him on the defensive. She understood, instinctively, that doing so might have alienated her from the all-male broker group. Making him angry wasn't the solution. Instead, she got his attention in a big way and in a language that he understood—drawing a firm line in the sand—and immediately diffused the situation with humor. He didn't take offense, and the meeting continued without further issue. None of the other all-male group members acknowledged what had occurred.

Today, that type of reaction might be risky, and we would not recommend any physical contact in retaliation other than maybe to push him away and let him know not to try that again or you will let his boss know how he spends his hours at work. The last thing a victim needs is to be blamed for sexual harassment herself. Whether the broker was hitting on JR, trying to be funny, or trying to rattle her, incidents like that were frequent throughout her career. Discouraging such behavior immediately was critical.

In another meeting in which JR was the only woman present, a cobroker working with her on a transaction was fired by the client for his lack of responsiveness to client inquiries. In a briefing on the situation, her fired cobroker lashed out at her in front of her boss and several male colleagues, saying, "This client likes you because you have tits and I don't!"

JR didn't hesitate to fire back. "The reason the client has confidence in me is because of my competence, responsiveness, and integrity. And by the way, anytime you want to exchange my tits for your dick, let's do it! I am confident that your dick has gotten you farther in this business than my tits!"

The guys in the room roared with laughter at her quick response. His deflection, however, was troubling. He did not want the group to focus on why the client fired him or that the client trusted JR's competence and ability more than his. He had a bruised ego and chose to decline his own responsibility for losing the client.

# A Sobering Reality Check
# Regarding Women's Right to Equality

Until the #MeToo movement launched, perception regarding the pervasiveness of sexual harassment appeared inconsistent. "Sexual harassment is no longer a big problem." "Young women today are better prepared to deal with sexual harassment when they join the workforce." "Our young men today are raised better." "HR is capable of properly handling sexual harassment claims, especially at large companies." We heard these statements repeatedly for years from strangers, friends, and colleagues, and we disagreed with them, which in part prompted our desire to write this book. Then came the #MeToo movement, and a wonderful uproar followed in almost every industry. Our purpose for this book became very relevant.

We also hear frequently that "women's rights have come a long way." Of course, this is true in many respects. Today, in the United States, women enjoy the right to vote, an identity outside of their husbands, health-care rights, birth control, equal education, the ability to affect policy, property ownership, the right to divorce, and the right to protective restraining orders. These are rights that strong female predecessors fought hard to obtain and that our current generation inherited. We should not take them for granted.

But have women's rights really come far enough? Let's review a few examples from a very male-dominated industry.

With approximately 1.3 million active workforce members, the US military is the largest employer in the world, but women comprise only 15 percent of military personnel. In the marine corps, women account for the smallest number of personnel—only about 9 percent, compared to just under 19 percent in the air force and 18 percent in the navy.[3] Women are difficult to recruit due to the military's toxic, misogynistic macho culture. If you need a refresher, "misogynism" is defined by Wikipedia as "the hatred of, contempt for, or prejudice against women or girls. Misogyny can be manifested in numerous ways, including social exclusion, sex discrimination, hostility, androcentrism, patriarchy, male privilege, belittling of women, violence against women, and sexual objectification."[4] In the military, the mental and physical training and the bonding rituals are male oriented and often extreme to promote the ideal warrior mind-set, which clashes with the traditional male view of women as the weaker sex.[5] I grew up in the military as the daughter of a NATO[6] intelligence officer in the German air force, and the servicewomen I met were highly competitive, intelligent, and tough, both mentally and physically. They were role models for me, and I admired their sense of confidence and strength. I witnessed how some of these servicewomen were treated by their male counterparts, and I understood at an early age that serving in the military as a woman required extraordinary patience, resilience, and strength. Regardless of a woman's ability to perform and compete in training, the traditional male view of women as a weaker gender prevails, and women who enter the armed forces continue to be unfairly tested by their male counterparts and superiors.

Sexual harassment and assault—and retaliation for reporting it—remains a serious problem in the military. After a series of sexual misconduct scandals rocked the military in 2013, the Joint Chiefs of Staff were summoned to give testimony before Congress on the issue of whether the military justice system was too antiquated to handle the problem of sexual harassment and assault. This was back in 2013, five years ago at time of writing. The Joint Chiefs acknowledged that the problem had been neglected for years and promised to devote new resources to training and law enforcement. In April 2018, the Pentagon released a new report noting that the number of sexual harassment complaints had jumped by 16 percent, and the number of sexual assault complaints had jumped from 6,172 in 2016 to 6,769 in fiscal year that ended September 30, 2017—a 10 percent increase, the highest number since the United States military began tracking reports more than a decade ago. The increase is claimed to be due to broader confidence in leadership and response action to hold violators accountable. However, only one in three victims files a claim, and most cases are handled quietly, behind closed doors.[7]

The 2018 Pentagon report also noted an increase in complaints of retaliation from 84 in 2016 to 146 in 2017. "Fear of ostracism and retaliation remains a barrier to reporting sexual assault or filing a sexual harassment complaint," the report said, adding that many women fear it will damage their reputations and haunt them for the length of their careers.[8]

To effect real change, successful female recruiting will require the military to overhaul its training to become gender neutral and allow sex crimes to be reported outside the chain of command, in military or civilian courts, with a transparent, consistent process. It's fair to ask how far along we've come toward that goal, and the answer is not far—definitely not far enough. Here are a few case examples:

A 2015 case involving Maxwell-Gunter Air Force Base is another indicator of lack of progress. In that case, it didn't matter to the commanding officer that a young female officer was repeatedly sexually harassed by a superior through inappropriate texts, emails, and videos (including video recordings of himself masturbating) repeatedly demanding sex, all of which were provided during the investigation. It didn't matter to the commanding officer that air force investigators confirmed her accounts when she finally reported the abuse. Despite the fact that military law allows for court martial and a sentence of up to seven years for this type of abuse, that same law also permits the commanding officer to determine if a criminal case should be pursued, and the commander here declined. Instead, he decided to impose nonjudicial discipline for conduct unbecoming of an officer. After subsequent challenge of the commander's determination and a new investigative review, the alleged violator was demoted one rank and forced to resign—with a full pension. Yes, a full pension.

In an effort to remove the prosecution of felonies, including sexual assaults, from commanders (who are often perpetrators themselves) to experienced military prosecutors, senator Kirsten Gillibrand reintroduced the Military Justice Improvement Act.[9] According to Gillibrand, sexual harassment and assault remain pervasive in the military despite years of efforts and minor reforms, and "top officials in the military continue to assert that they alone will fix this, but little has changed."[10] After receiving support of a bipartisan majority of senators for the second straight Congress, the act was filibustered again.[11]

Another, and more shocking, story broke in January 2017. Marine veteran Thomas Brennan, who runs a nonprofit news organization called the War Horse, uncovered scandalous activity on the "Marines United" Facebook page, launched in 2015 with membership limited to only male marines, navy corpsmen, and British Royal Marines. When the web page was exposed, it featured hundreds of posts in which female marines were disparaged, made the subject of vile and sexually inappropriate comments, and displayed in explicit pictures, sparking outrage.[12] A joint military task force comprised of air force, army, coast guard, marine, and navy investigators was formed to jointly investigate the culture that gave rise to Marines United's Facebook posts, to develop and implement corrective changes to policies and procedures, and to modify education and training to help prevent any such activity in the future.[13] The task force was created in early 2017, and according to recent reporting, few changes have been made to reform the misogynist culture.[14]

In the military, women's rights have not come far enough.

Early last year, right after the well-attended Women's March in Philadelphia, a Facebook post appeared that started with, "I am not a 'disgrace to women' because I don't support the women's march . . . [and] . . . I do not feel I am a 'second-class citizen' because I am a woman."[15] This post was shared by many women who felt criticized and shamed for not attending the Women's March in Philadelphia or in other cities around the country, claiming they felt *equal enough* to men and that, as women, they felt *they had come plenty far* concerning women's rights. We agree with Dina Leygerman's response to the above post, a blog post she published on Facebook titled "You Are Not Equal. I'm Sorry."[16] Her article spoke to the extent of "equality" of women concerning human rights. In this country, women's rights have not yet come far enough. Women are still lobbying for the right to make decisions about when to terminate a pregnancy, the right to breastfeed in public, the right to be paid maternity leave for a reasonable period of time (such as six weeks or more), the right to certain health care and medications (including for contraception), and the right to walk the streets and join the workforce without the threat of sexual harassment. With respect to women's rights in the Sandbox of the workplace, women are not equal enough to men when it comes to the right to equal jobs, equal promotions, equal pay for equal work, and a workplace free of bullying, discrimination, and sexual harassment. According to the sources referenced in Leygerman's blog, the US ranks forty-fifth in inequality concerning women's rights—behind Rwanda, Cuba, the Philippines, and Jamaica.[17]

## Supporting Feminism Is Not a Negative: The True Meaning

We must continue fighting for equal rights for women. Whether you are a man or a woman, this means supporting and embracing feminism. In some circles, the term *feminism* is viewed negatively. In others, if you are not an activist fighting aggressively for women's rights, you are not a true feminist. You may even be decried as "antifeminist" and not worthy of respect. Let's review the definition. According to *Merriam-Webster*, the term *feminism* means "the theory of the political, economic, and social equality of the sexes."[18] Vocabulary.com says, "A feminist is someone who supports equal rights for women [politically, socially, and economically]. If your brother objects strongly to women being paid less than men for doing the same job, he's probably a feminist." This website provides further that "it has absolutely nothing to do with putting down men or boys in order to elevate the status of women."[19] In other words, feminism means that you believe that men and women should have equal rights and opportunities, including in the workforce. It absolutely does not mean that we must hate men or decry all things masculine. It does not mean that we have to "act like a bitch" to be heard, walk around angry, use foul language, or spew hate speech when we communicate with others. It does not mean that we should act or dress like men. It does not mean that we should hate the color pink and never dress pretty.[20] Feminism is a very important cause, we believe, intended to promote equal rights for all women socially, economically, and politically. Voting liberal or conservative should not mean you are less of a feminist. In our view, supporting feminism should be bipartisan and nonpolitical and should be championed by all women and all men who support women. JR and I are influencing the men in our lives to be diehard feminists. Eliminating sexual harassment permanently is an important milestone to achieving equal rights for women—especially in the Sandbox of the Playground of a company.

# 1

# Welcome to the Sandbox

## The Meaning of the Sandbox on the Playground of the Work Environment

The workplace culture for any business is valuable and should be carefully constructed, populated, and nourished. This workplace culture is part of the working environment JR and I have come to call the Playground of a business. The term *playground* is used so we can apply the "playground rules" that we will review later in this book. The Sandbox in this playground is where we imagine men and women work, collaborate, receive mentorship, develop ideas and products, and create and complete projects and where the success of any business is ultimately measured. The Sandbox should be a key focus: a positive and healthy environment populated by both men and women who are a complement of strengths and weaknesses and in a varied culture of diversity. The Sandbox should have leadership that commands mutual respect, promotes healthy mentorship, and demands an environment free of bigotry, gender bias, and sexual harassment. If the Sandbox fails in any of those respects, the health and success of the business are likely to suffer adverse consequences and negatively impact the financial bottom line. Recent news headlines regarding the high dollar amount of settlements alone (regarding, for example, Fox News) continue to underscore this premise. Unfortunately, in the many years JR and I have been in the workforce, sexual harassment has continued.

## Company Policies and Current Legislation Are Not Sufficient

JR and I have been talking about sexual harassment in the workplace since we first met, and we firmly believe efforts to date, including policies and procedures against such behavior in the workplace, have done little to deter sexual harassment. The explosion of the #MeToo movement involving almost every industry puts to rest any doubts.

Let's review a recent news example involving our elected officials.

In late 2017 and early 2018, the US House of Representatives held a riveting hearing wherein lawmakers heard "witnesses [tell] stories of House Congressional members grabbing accusers' genitals on the House floor, disrobing in front of a female staffer late at night, and propositioning staffers by asking things like, 'Are you going to be a good girl?'"[1] According to reports published at the time, US Congressional employees are subject to a lengthy and intimidating process if they want to file a sexual harassment complaint. First, they must participate in a thirty-day counseling period about the incident and then a thirty-day mediation period with the abuser. If the matter settles, any settlement payments are confidential and paid from a special US Treasury fund—yes, from our tax dollars instead of from the accused's funds—and the accuser is required to sign a confidentiality agreement to keep the resolution private. "Like Hollywood, . . . the Capitol Hill environment is dominated by powerful men who can make or break careers."[2]

The news regarding the process and payments made to date from our tax dollars triggered national anger. In response, US Senator Gillibrand and others worked on a bipartisan Senate bill to change the process for filing claims and to provide transparency regarding the terms of a settlement. The goal was to remove the part of the process that "silences" the victims and keeps the abuser, the proceedings, and the fees paid a government secret. Another goal was to prohibit settlements from using the US Treasury fund and taxpayer dollars. In February of 2018, House Republicans and Democrats actually passed a bipartisan bill to overhaul the process and handling of investigating sexual harassment claims on Capitol Hill. The new House bill amended the Congressional Accountability Act of 1995 [H.R.4924 & H.Res.724] to provide more transparency, eliminate the mandatory thirty-day counseling and mediation periods, and require members of Congress to repay any settlements paid from the Treasury within ninety days.[3] When the bill had yet to be passed by the Senate on March 28, 2018, all twenty-two female senators—Republicans and Democrats— demanded that the Senate take bipartisan effort to create a similar bill.[4] Finally, the Senate approved its own bipartisan bill, which eliminates any mandatory counseling, mediation, and "cooling off" periods victims are currently required to endure before filing a lawsuit or requesting an administrative hearing and which requires any settlements to be repaid to the Treasury. The bill is now headed back to the House, but not without criticism.[5] To name a few criticisms, the requirement to repay settlements relates only to sexual harassment (excluding discrimination), and further review by the congressional ethics committee is required of any settlement to decide if an investigation is necessary to determine whether the member engaged in sexual harassment and should be required to repay the settlement amount to Treasury, providing possible opportunities for alleged violating members to escape accountability.[6]

Despite the institutional problems remaining, many politicians have suffered consequences as a result of sexual harassment allegations, exemplifying decades of bad behavior by several of them. Since the start of 2017, at least fourteen state legislators from ten US states have resigned from office following allegations of sexual harassment or misconduct, and at least sixteen others have faced other repercussions, such as voluntary or forced removal from their leadership positions. Approximately three-fourths of the states have at least one legislative chamber that has updated its sexual harassment policy, developed specific proposals to do so, or undertaken a review of whether changes are needed in response to the wave of revelations across the country out of state and local governmental bodies.[7]

Sexual harassment in and outside of the workplace is alive and well, and it is high time to effect changes that will make sexual harassment socially unacceptable and legally prohibited to an extent that violators are permanently deterred from assuming the risk of violation—whether at work, at social events and gatherings, on the street, or otherwise. Our current laws regarding sexual harassment do not reach beyond the work environment and are complicated. Here is a brief review.

Title VII of the Civil Rights Act of 1964[8] (herein called *Title VII*) makes sexual harassment perpetrated by men and women against federal law and requires employers with fifteen employees or more, including state and local governments, to provide a workplace environment free from any such harassment. Per 42 U.S.C. §2000e-2(a), Title VII provides that "it shall be an unlawful employment practice for an employer . . . to discriminate against any individual with respect to [her] . . . terms, conditions, or privileges of employment, because of such individual's . . . sex." In 1986, the Supreme Court ruled that discrimination with respect to the terms, conditions, or privileges of employment on the basis of sex includes sexual harassment, defined as "unwelcome sexual advances . . . and other . . . conduct of a sexual nature" and having the "purpose or effect of interfering with an individual's work performance or creating an intimidating, hostile or offensive working environment."[9]

In 1998, the Supreme Court clarified the scope of actionable sexual harassment in two landmark cases, Ellerth and Faragher.[10] In these cases, the court set a new standard[11] for establishing an employer's liability for sexual harassment perpetrated by a supervisor[12] through a determination of whether or not the employee suffered a "tangible employment action" in connection with gender-based, unwelcome conduct.[13] This meant a significant change in employment status, such as hiring, firing, failing to promote, reassignment with significantly different responsibilities, or a decision causing a significant change in benefits.[14] An example would be if the supervisor required his or her employee to perform a sex act for a raise or promotion (a "quid pro quo" action). Where there is no such "tangible employment action" (meaning the employee is still employed with no adverse change in the employee's status), the employer may still be liable for sexual harassment by a supervisor who creates a "hostile work environment." The environment must be one in which "discriminatory intimidation, ridicule, and insult . . . [are] sufficiently severe or pervasive as to alter the conditions of a victim's employment."[15] The "severe or pervasive" standard refers to extreme conduct,[16] severe meaning sexual assault and pervasive meaning repeated patterns of behavior, such as a male employee making lewd comments about a woman's body parts every time she walks by, or openly showing offensive pictures to women to get a reaction, or rubbing up against or standing too close to a female when they are alone. Isolated and occasional teasing, sexist jokes, and comments may not rise to the level of actionable sexual harassment unless the single, isolated incident is more serious (certain types of inappropriate touching or sexual assault).[17] Courts also apply the "reasonable person" standard to determine if the harassing conduct is sufficiently severe or pervasive as to alter the employee's terms and conditions of employment.[18] If the employee is seeking to hold the employer liable for a sexually hostile work environment, the employee is encouraged to first file a complaint with the company and endeavor to do so as promptly as possible.[19] The Ellerth and Faragher cases also establish affirmative defenses to employer liability for supervisor sexual harassment.[20]

Employers are also liable for sexual harassment committed by coworkers (who are not supervisors) and nonemployees (where the employer has control over such individual's misconduct) if the employer (or its agents or supervisory employees) knew or should have known of the misconduct, *unless* the employer can show that it took immediate and appropriate corrective action.[21]

The Equal Employment Opportunity Commission (or *EEOC*), defines sexual harassment more simply as follows: "Unwelcome sexual advances, requests for sexual favors, and other verbal or physical conduct of a sexual nature constitutes sexual harassment when submission to or rejection of this conduct explicitly or implicitly affects an individual's employment, unreasonably interferes with an individual's work performance or creates an intimidating, hostile or offensive work environment."[22] Sexual harassment can be perpetrated by a man or a woman,[23, 24] and sexual harassment does not necessarily have to be sexual. All that's required is that it be related to a person's gender in some way. For example, a fellow male employee referring to a female as "the girl" every time he sees or introduces her.[25]

Current laws should be less complicated and should apply to all persons regardless of whether they are in a work environment or not. We have waited far too long, and we must take advantage of the momentum of #MeToo and Time's Up and effect real and permanent change. The efforts of the Producer's Guild of America, the Time's Up Legal Defense Fund, Women in Film, and others, including certain politicians and celebrities (such as Gretchen Carlson) who have proposed new legislation, have been wonderful efforts for change.

The #MeToo and Time's Up movements are already having a positive impact and are likely going to trigger further changes to existing laws and to the policies and procedures of companies. But will these changes have an immediate positive effect to change the toxic, misogynistic workplace culture or to reduce the temptation to abuse power? Will there be an immediate impact on the promotion of collaboration, civility, and equality of respect between men and women and their behavior in the Sandbox? Until violators realize that the potential risks associated with sexual harassment outweigh the benefits, it will be up to all of us—the men and women in the Sandbox—to continue effecting change to stop this behavior.

The explosion of the #MeToo and Time's Up movements should have caused violators to worry about their careers, keep a low profile, and modify their behavior. You certainly would not expect a violator to publicly support the #MeToo movement. Here is one very recent high-profile example.

New York's attorney general, Eric Schneiderman, championed the #MeToo movement by using his position to sue Hollywood director Harvey Weinstein, demanding greater compensation for his alleged victims.[26] When the *Times* and the *New Yorker* were awarded a joint Pulitzer Prize for coverage of sexual harassment, Schneiderman sent a congratulatory tweet honoring those who spoke up: "Without the reporting of the @nytimes and the @newyorker—and the brave women and men who spoke up about the sexual harassment they endured at the hands of powerful men—there would not be the critical national reckoning underway. A well-deserved honor."[27] Since that time, Schneiderman has himself been accused by four women of sexual misconduct and nonconsensual physical violence and has resigned from office effective as of May 8, 2018.[28]

Businesses across all industries should be testing their work cultures and making any needed changes, including to their policies and procedures, to correct objectionable behavior. However, despite the current movements and the potential for serious consequences, sexual abuse continues. Every day, new incidents are being reported in the news and on social media that evidence in part a lack of understanding by violators (and potentially by bystanders) of what constitutes inappropriate behavior. Let's take Morgan Freeman, one of our most favorite actors, as an example. Some of his famous roles include parts in *Driving Miss Daisy*, *The Shawshank Redemption*, and *Million Dollar Baby*. Freeman has now been accused of inappropriate behavior on many of his movie sets for years, including sexual comments about body parts and clothes and inappropriate touching.[29] What is troubling is that Freeman does not believe his behavior was inappropriate and sexual harassment. Freeman released a statement saying that he is devastated at the accusations and that his behavior was not with intent to harm, noting further that "it is not right to equate horrific incidents of sexual assault with misplaced compliments or humor . . . I would often try to joke with and compliment women, in what I thought was a light-hearted and humorous way. Clearly I was not always coming across the way I intended. . . . But I also want to be clear: I did not create unsafe work environments. I did not assault women. I did not offer employment or advancement in exchange for sex. Any suggestion that I did so is completely false."[30] From his statement, one thing is very obvious. He does not appreciate the meaning and implications of sexual harassment. Although Freeman has publicly apologized several times, his behavior has triggered serious consequences. Advertisers who use his powerful voice, including Visa, have suspended commercials where the actor is featured.[31]

Another recent case involves Louis C.K., a comedian well known for his roles in *Parks and Recreation* and *Louie*. C.K. was also accused of inappropriate behavior dating back more than a decade according to five women, including masturbating in front of them even when confronted and told to stop. By late 2017, Louis's New York premiere of his upcoming movie, *I Love You, Daddy*, and his appearance on *The Late Show with Stephen Colbert* were both abruptly canceled just prior to the news breaking about his sexual deviancy.[32] Louis C.K. has since admitted to the alleged conduct and expressed remorse for taking advantage of his influence "irresponsibly."

As Oprah Winfrey recently stated at the 2018 Golden Globes, we must strive to reach a point "when nobody ever has to say 'me too' again." We agree. As a society, we must act and help educate violators as to what is not appropriate behavior and how to "unlearn" acts of sexual harassment. We must help women gain the confidence to address and defend against sexual harassment immediately when it occurs, especially where such behavior is frequent and common.

Where the Sandbox is populated predominantly with men (which is the reality for many businesses), setting expectations and boundaries for appropriate behavior is important. Relying on HR to correct each instance is not a realistic option. In our view, violations are simply too frequent, and if you work at a company where each division or transaction is populated with a different group of men and you also deal with noncompany persons, such as customers and vendors, who are men, HR may not be able to process your complaints in a timely or effective manner or even have any control over the third parties. Violations occur outside of work as well and must be dealt with in a similar fashion.

Let's take a recent example from the tech industry. Uber is hailed as one of the most successful startup tech companies of its time in Silicon Valley. Uber's creators developed an app that shook the taxi industry, allowing customers to call a ride with ease and efficiency and allowing drivers to work and earn extra income on a convenient, flexible schedule. Today, Uber has an estimated sixteen thousand employees worldwide, in 616 cities and seventy-seven countries, and is worth approximately $69 billion in US dollars.[33]

Despite its impressive success, Uber also had a tumultuous 2017, with conflicts plaguing the company, including battles with city regulators and the US Department of Justice, lawsuits filed by Google's parent company claiming technology trademark violations, rape and sexual assault allegations against some of its drivers, drivers' classification and benefits, and claims by competitor Lyft of engaging in tactics of sabotage. Uber's legal troubles arguably only exploded, however, when Susan J. Fowler, an Uber engineer, published a blog post on February 19, 2017, about her treatment at Uber. In her blog, she exposed that Uber suffers from a workplace culture unfriendly to women, causing a shake-up of the tech industry.[34] Fowler joined Uber as an engineer in November 2015, and after beginning her training, she was almost immediately propositioned for sex by her manager through a string of messages over company chat—clearly inappropriate behavior for a manager, especially when using company resources. Despite her prompt report to Uber's HR department, HR did not take any serious disciplinary action. Instead, even though HR acknowledged the manager's behavior was inappropriate, Fowler was repeatedly told all the company could do was give the offender a stern warning. According to Fowler's blog, upper management said the offender was a "high performer," and they didn't want to ruin his career over his "first offense" or "an innocent mistake" on his part. HR advised Fowler to either move teams to avoid interacting with him or to stay—a scenario in which she would likely suffer from poor performance reviews, which HR did not view as retaliation (since she had the option to change teams).

Let's take a quick pause here. *What?* Uber is a modern-day, state-of-the-art company populated with a generation of well-educated young people, and their HR department would not take any action? Fowler soon found out from other women at the company that her old manager had previously harassed other female engineers, that such behavior was continuing, and that HR and upper management knew about it and chose to ignore it. HR had apparently lied—and so had upper management—about Fowler's case being a "first offense." Fowler had no choice but to leave the company after her efforts for promotion were thereafter blocked despite (she believed) her stellar performance reviews and work accomplishments.

So Fowler left the company and published her blog, and the fallout was both fast and furious. Uber hired former US attorney general Eric H. Holder Jr. to investigate and make recommendations about how Uber should address and remediate its workplace culture. The investigations of more than two hundred claims of sexual harassment and other workplace misconduct resulted in the firing of twenty employees and the reprimanding of more than forty additional employees.[35] Uber's board of directors promptly adopted Holder's lengthy recommendations, including new performance reviews to hold senior leaders accountable; increased diversity; enhanced oversight, expansion, and training of the HR department; extensive revamping of sexual harassment policies and procedures; reformation of Uber's cultural values; implementation of more rigorous restrictions on use and consumption of alcohol at company events; restrictions regarding romantic relationships between employees; removal of employee job transfer barriers; and employee retention initiatives.[36] Soon after that, Uber's CEO, Travis Kalanick, agreed to take a leave of absence of undetermined length after pressure from Uber's largest investors. It was an incredible fall from grace for a "tech visionary" like Kalanick, who, according to the *New York Times*, "had transformed the global transportation industry with Uber's ride-hailing service and pushed the company's value to nearly $70 billion, making it the most highly valued startup in the world."[37]

However, despite popular perception, Uber is not the first Silicon Valley or startup tech firm to face allegations of sexual harassment and discrimination. It's been reported, and backed by a number of studies, that Silicon Valley "maintains a reputation for inhospitality to women, people of color, [and] anyone who did not go to an Ivy League school." One such study "found that women leave tech jobs at twice the rate men do" and that "half or more [women] reported being asked to do menial tasks men aren't expected to, dealing with unwanted sexual advances and feeling they don't have the opportunities as their male counterparts."[38]

So, why is the bad behavior of "high performers" tolerated? Is the dollar value of their work performance worth more than the risk of potential sexual harassment liability to the company? What was the ultimate impact of Fowler's blog on Uber, whether financial or otherwise? We understand from reports that Uber lost some market share to Lyft and that there have been financial losses.[39] Regardless of how companies may be publicly interpreting their financial reports, we hope that Uber's plight has given the tech industry a renewed focus to take decisive action to improve their current culture of discrimination and sexual harassment and to move toward achieving diversity.

Members of HR departments are often uncomfortable disciplining a high performer and/or too fearful of losing their own jobs to do so, especially if the alleged violator is in a position of power, an executive, or popular within the company. Managers and HR departments need proper training on how to communicate with, handle, and punish perpetrators in a swift and consistent manner regardless of their position. The implementation of zero-tolerance policies against any form of sexual harassment and discrimination is a prerequisite for a chance at efficiently discouraging bad behavior, regardless of the level of violation and regardless of the status of a perpetrator as a high performer.

Drastic changes are both needed and critical. To this day, women are still reluctant to report their abusers—and with excellent reason. It does not matter whether the abused female is a low-ranking staffer, a contributing associate, an employee with rank, or a well-known personality. If the abuser has a superior position, is a high performer, or is a person with influence, he or she has the power to make or break a subordinate's career, and sometimes even those of female peers. If you dare to report the abuser, you are likely to suffer retaliation in the form of negative work reviews, loss of social group interaction, discrimination, public humiliation and harassment, loss of work opportunities, demotion, denial of bonuses and raises, assignment of menial tasks, transfer to a lower-income job, being fired or laid off, or being forced to leave, directly or (often) indirectly.

The tech industry is seeking to actively make changes concerning sexual harassment and diversity, including a bill seeking to prohibit sexual harassment in the venture capital industry explicitly between entrepreneurs and potential investors, which are relationships not currently covered by employment laws.[40] However, progress is slow. According to recent reporting, the National Venture Capital Association—comprised of industry leaders—spent the greater part of 2017 working with law firms, HR specialists, and venture partners to establish guidelines and best practices for education and training around sexual harassment, including suggested policies and procedures. However, the results of the association's efforts have not been released, so it's unclear what progress has even been made.[41]

## The Importance of Self-Help and the Rules of the Playground

Until businesses and organizations can implement and enforce effective policies and procedures with appropriately trained and empowered HR staff, and until existing laws are appropriately improved and/or enacted with sufficiently severe consequences to stop sexual harassment once and for all, women and men need to take self-help action to modify bad behavior and encourage good behavior—immediately when the objectionable behavior occurs. Our approach in dealing with sexual harassment "on the spot" is to implement what we call Plan A—an action plan and guiding rules for discussion that we believe will help modify bad behavior. Plan A is likely to promote a better working relationship with your counterparts, superiors, and clients and will give you the opportunity to educate family members, colleagues, superiors, and friends on how to be more sensitive and respectful when interacting. We further believe that Plan A will help teach them how to effect change as a bystander when they witness bullying, discrimination, and sexual misconduct, without fear of retaliation or risking their careers. We are a modern, civilized society. Let's reintroduce civility, respect, and compassion and help violators unlearn bad behavior.

Before we jump in to the details of Plan A and the related guiding rules with respect to the working environment, let's discuss where awareness, discussion, and education on the topics of sexual harassment, bullying, and discrimination should begin, where exposure occurs at an early age, and which environments should discourage but continue to breed bad behavior prior to entering the workforce.

# 2

# Where Does Bad Behavior Start, and Where Should We Begin to Effect Change?

## Education at Home, Middle School, and High School

There are theories that boys learn how to harass girls at an early age by watching the patterns of male behavior at home and in their community.[1] The stories they read, the television shows and cartoons they enjoy, and even the action figures they play with emphasize that males are "supposed" to have power and authority, including over females. As boys mature, they exercise this power through disruptive and harassing behavior at school and on the playground, often excused as "boys will be boys."[2]

When you were in middle school, did you see boys snap a shoulder strap on a girl's bra, or lift her skirt, or grab her breast? You would look around for the culprit, and a group of boys would run away laughing? How did the girl react? Did she run after them and set them straight, or did she feel more comfortable changing her behavior to wear shorts under her skirt and walk the halls with a book held firmly to her chest? What about today? Are our children bold enough to report such behavior, or are they too embarrassed or ashamed and make adjustments to avoid such behavior? What about bullying and discrimination? What are our educational institutions doing to address these types of behaviors with students? Are they teaching our students how to combat and stop this type of behavior when it occurs? Are the penalties imposed by our schools severe enough to deter repeat behavior?

What about what young men learn from their male family members and role models?

Before we review what is happening outside of the home, take a good look at what your kids are exposed to in your household. If you are a married couple with children, are you treating each other with love and respect? Are you mindful of how you communicate and express frustration? Your children are watching how you interact and may be influenced to copy your actions as good behavior. Are you raising your voices and addressing each other in a disrespectful tone of voice? Be aware of your own unconscious gender biases. We all have them. It should be OK for girls to play with cars and video games and for boys to learn how to bake a cake. Boys should be able to cry and share their emotions. Encouraging sensitivity does not make a boy weak. How else will you know what is going on with your son? How else will you be able to teach him how to work through a difficult situation? We also believe it is OK for girls to get dirty and play flag football with the boys. How would girls otherwise learn how to effectively communicate with and handle boys their age?

As parents, consider sharing household chores without bias. Dads can vacuum carpets, and moms can clean out gutters. There is no shame in a guy getting on his hands and knees to scrub a floor or clean a toilet. Learning how to change a tire at a young age will help a young woman be independent if she gets stranded (and will certainly impress the boys). Making labor chores more gender neutral is likely to foster respect between boys and girls when they interact. Maybe your son will be less likely to demean certain tasks, and maybe your daughter will handle certain tasks more confidently. It is important to learn how to handle bad behavior not only for girls; boys also need to determine what is appropriate and what is not, how to discourage such behavior when they see it, and how to help their sisters and peers when they are being harassed or bullied. Most importantly, our children need to learn how to combat peer pressure with natural and realistic tools and how to develop healthy character guidelines and a robust belief system. Parameters of appropriate behavior and self-respect are critical in helping our children shape who they are or will become as they mature into young adults.

Many parents are reluctant to start this education when their children are young. They want to keep their children sheltered from controversial issues and avoid discussion when sexual incidents occur at school or make national news. Know, however, that if you fail to have these discussions in a controlled environment, you risk your children resolving their concerns with their peers or other adults without proper guidance from you, as their parents, or, if appropriate, from applicable experts. In terms of age, you will have to decide what is best for your child and family. Some experts say to start when your children are just beginning school, most likely in kindergarten.[3] As the parents of two daughters, we (the Kimichiks) made it a priority to discuss important issues as they arose, often straight from current news headlines. We would let our daughters read a news story or address an issue that occurred at school and then encourage discussion. It was important to hear how they felt about the subject. I even made them watch *Law & Order* episodes relevant to bullying, hazing, and sexual assault (often stories ripped straight from the newspapers). We started educating our girls at an early age, usually at the dinner table, and continue this practice today. One is in college and the other in graduate school. I like to say that we flung as much out there as we could, hoping maybe some of it would stick and make an impression.

Education starts at home. We cannot rely solely on schools, teachers, and peers to do this very important job, for education on the topics of sexual harassment and proper behavior may not be available (or may not be, in substance, as we would address them). We must also pay attention to what our children access on television, computers, tablets, and phones, including pornography. Parental monitoring, intervention, education, and frequent discussion regarding sensitive topics is paramount. If your children are still at home, find a time for family discussion at least a few times a week, at dinner time, without any phones or disruptive electronic devices. Consider putting all phones in a basket far away from the dinner table. Talk about what is going on at school and in the news. Perhaps most importantly, encourage your children to express their opinions, and listen to what they have to say. Be gentle with your opinions and guidance, and don't be judgmental. You want the discussions to be a positive learning experience for them. You want them to look forward to and enjoy your dinners, not dread them.

We have talked to many parents of younger children and have been surprised to learn that many don't think sexual harassment and assault are current problems in our schools. They may say that "we have come a long way" or that "that doesn't happen anymore" or that "our new generation of young boys and girls doesn't have to worry about sexual harassment and assault." Or, maybe most commonly: "We've raised our boys and girls better, and our schools are educating our children to be aware and defend against such behavior!" These are strong statements and may not be entirely accurate.

Let's look at a very recent example. Four male teens showed up at a high school "pink out" football game (the school's annual Breast Cancer Awareness Night), bare chested, each with a pink letter sprayed on his chest. They stood together and then posted a picture on social media with the comment "What we do to Daniel," referring to the opposing football team. The letters spelled "RAPE."[4] How is it possible that these young men would think it's alright to joke about rape as a viable threat at any event, much less at a school event fundraiser for breast cancer awareness? Are we, as parents, discussing these issues at home with our young adults? The #MeToo movement is giving us plenty to talk about at the dinner table. The school claims to have disciplined these young men, but they were not expelled. Will the punishment they received deter this type of behavior when they get to college or start their first job? The school would not disclose the form of punishment, so it leaves us to wonder what was and will be the real result.[5]

If you are bothered by the prevalence of sexual harassment in our workforce, you will be disturbed to learn how much more severe these issues are in our high schools, colleges, and universities. The statistics are terrifying and primarily involve sexual assault and rape perpetrated by children and young adults.[6] Here are a few examples.

On January 18, 2018, a sixteen-year-old Palo Verde High School student was indicted by a grand jury. He was accused of raping at least four teenage classmates while he was a student at a prior high school, Shadow Ridge High School, from which he had been previously expelled.[7] In another case, hundreds of students walked out of classes at McClatchy High School in Sacramento, California, on March 21, 2018, to protest how school officials handled sexual harassment claims. One of those claims involved an alleged gang rape at an off-campus party in May 2016. The student claimed she was drugged and raped by two other students while she was unconscious and was filmed passed out on the bed without her pants.[8]

In a case involving social media, Facebook Live broadcast a video of a fifteen-year-old girl being gang-raped in Chicago by as many as six people. At one point, at least forty people were watching the livestream, but no one called the police.[9] Of the six perpetrators, only two boys, ages fourteen and fifteen, have been located and arrested in connection with the rape and charged with aggravated criminal assault, manufacturing of child pornography, and dissemination of child pornography. Despite the severity of the crime, the teenagers must be prosecuted in Chicago's juvenile court system, and a determination must be made by the court whether they are to be tried as minors or adults.[10] These are not isolated incidents. It's heartbreaking that our children are exposed to sexual harassment, assault, and bullying not only in our schools but also in our homes on social media. The impact is devastating, especially to the victims, and can lead to lifelong scars and, in many cases, suicide.[11]

## Education in Preparation for College or University

If that doesn't shake you to your core, once our children graduate from high school, the potential for bullying, hazing, sexual harassment, assault, and rape continues in colleges and universities. This is in addition to the risks of drug and alcohol abuse. The recent case examples are just as horrifying and disturbing. Every few weeks in the headlines, new incidents surface at both public and private colleges and universities, and even the most elite are no exception, despite recent incidents that have focused national attention on much-needed changes. One striking example involves Timothy Piazza, a freshman at Pennsylvania State University, who died during a Beta Theta Pi fraternity pledge initiation called "the Gauntlet." According to reports, he was served eighteen drinks in roughly an hour and a half, and, not able to walk on his own, he fell several times, including down a flight of stairs, causing numerous injuries. Members of the fraternity did not seek medical attention until the next morning. Piazza died February 4, 2017.[12] His death was the first of four pledge deaths across the country, sparking a national conversation about the rituals and benefits of hazing activities. Affected universities are taking "antihazing measures" (including banning certain fraternities and implementing rules regarding alcohol use at parties), and the US Senate recently passed the Timothy J. Piazza Anti-Hazing Bill (in large part due to the persistent efforts of

Timothy Piazza's parents). Of the twenty-six people originally charged in connection with Piazza's death, to date one has pleaded guilty to four counts of hazing. [13]

Educating our children should start at home and within our family, social, and community circles. Both men and women must participate. How we communicate and treat one another is important to establish role-model behavior for our younger generations.

When I was getting my oldest daughter ready for college, I insisted she take self-defense classes in case she ever needed to protect herself. She thought I was being ridiculous and declared, "Sexual assault does not occur on the campus of my university!" We compromised by first studying the statistics before continuing the self-defense class discussion. Unfortunately, as we discovered, the issue exists at almost every college and university campus across the country, and it became more important to understand whether the university in question had proper and effective procedures in place to help if a sexual assault did, in fact, occur.

As a result, both of our daughters (and several of their friends) took self-defense classes before they went to college. Yes, we did get some, "Ugh, Mom, do we have to?" and a lot of eye rolling, but I think today they'd tell you our efforts made them better prepared to handle certain situations—or at least gave them a chance to consider options. The self-defense classes taught them how to communicate boundaries with simple words and gestures. Saying, "Back up, you're in my space!" or stretching out a hand to move the person a few feet away became second nature. My oldest daughter later reported one incident where she was pushed up against a wall by a drunk fraternity brother at a party. She did not hesitate to use her hand to push him away and establish distance. The self-defense classes taught them not to be afraid to push back and use force if necessary. They became more alert about their surroundings, and traveling with a buddy late at night was reinforced as an important protective measure.

If you have not seen the CNN special *The Hunting Ground*, first aired in a two-part series November 22, 2015, *please* make the time—especially if you have daughters. In fact, if your daughters are about to go to college, encourage them to watch this special (which you can find through your cable provider on demand, through Netflix, or online) with their classmates, and then invite open discussion with a few then college students who are willing to share some of their own recent experiences. If you can get their male classmates to join, even better! This CNN special reviews the prevalence and typical scenarios of sexual assault on our campuses and tells the story of how two young women traveled to universities across the country to help student survivors of rape and sexual assault file Title IX actions against their universities.[14] These actions forced schools to implement proper resources for reporting sexual assault and protection as well as accountability programs regarding reporting of incidents of sexual assault and appropriate punishment, including criminal prosecution and permanent expulsion.

Current efforts, however, are not really changing the behavior landscape. Shocking incidents continue to make the news almost every month, and colleges and universities are not learning from them despite agreement on the urgent need for change. At many colleges and universities, school officials are concerned that taking action might harm athletic programs and/or donor funding efforts. Baylor and Vanderbilt Universities are just a couple of campuses with notorious stories about sexual assault and rape and how those claims were handled (or, more accurately, mishandled). In just early 2017, more than 220 schools faced sexual harassment investigations.[15]

These days, in college, casual sex without commitment to a relationship is much more in vogue and acceptable, and it is critically important to appreciate the intent or state of mind of your partner. If you don't, you may risk ruining your future and, potentially, your life. Alcohol, peer pressure, and the victim's dress (or lack thereof) or reputation around campus are not evidence of permission for inter-course. If a potential partner says no or is incapable of giving consent because they are intoxicated or passed out, you may be committing assault and violating the law. As parents, it is imperative that we teach our children at home what constitutes inappropriate behavior and how to reduce the risk of being a target or becoming a violator. This same concern exists for hazing activities. Make it a point to discuss the importance of morality, integrity, respect for the opposite sex, sound judgment, and what behavior violates our laws. Do it yourself. Do not rely on others or assume they are rendering this very important educa-tion. If you don't know or are uncomfortable finding a way to address these controversial topics, just collect a few stories from the headlines. There are plenty of recent examples to talk about.

Baylor University's recent troubles involving sexual assault com-mitted by multiple members of its football team (including several gang rapes) over many years—and the alleged knowledge of this by the football program, school officials, and even the local police force without pursuit and prosecution of claims—is just one of many horrifying examples. According to Baylor regents, seventeen women reported sexual or domestic assaults involving nineteen players, including four gang rapes, since 2011. No action was taken. This is especially troubling for Baylor, a longtime haven for Christian families seeking a sheltered collegiate environment for their daughters and sons. Premarital sex and alcohol are prohibited by the Baylor student code of conduct.[16] Many argue that protecting the football program and its players and maintaining donor funding was more important than the health and safety of women. There was fallout. Baylor president Ken Starr (the special prosecutor whose investigation led to the 1998 impeachment of US president Bill Clinton) was first demoted and then eventually resigned; football coach Art Briles was fired; and athletic director Ian McCaw resigned. Several players have been found guilty, and one was sentenced to twenty years in prison. Several more lawsuits are pending.[17]

We must teach our children appropriate behavior, how to set boundaries and defend against bad acts, and how to be confident to stand up for themselves and their friends, but, understandably, we often find ourselves too busy to find quality time to engage in meaningful discussions with our children about important topics. If we fail to do so, however, they may be negatively influenced by their peers in ways we don't and can't understand if we haven't been communicating with them regularly. As they enter middle school, high school, and college, they may have a distorted view of what type of behavior is acceptable or appropriate or what they think they must tolerate or endure. They will succumb to peer pressure as opposed to following their consciences and the belief systems they learned at home. The preceding applies to both boys and girls, as they can both be victims and offenders.

In addition to starting early at home in educating our children, we also need our schools (starting with middle schools) to implement policies against sexual harassment and assault with adequate penalties for violators and to educate staff and students regarding sexual violence, inappropriate behavior, and defending against predators. Every high school should provide an opportunity to take self-defense classes to prepare for college. If not in high school, self-defense classes, along with seminars on alcohol abuse, bullying, discrimination, hazing, and sexual harassment, should be mandatory for every student entering college in the first few weeks of their freshman semester. Online mandatory seminars may not be sufficient. Interactive sessions with experts several times a year might have more of an impact to changing objectionable and illegal behavior. Learning how to physically respond to bad acts with confidence will go a long way toward protecting our boys and girls—first when they get to college and then when they join the workforce (the Sandbox). If not, what they learn in their early years, at home, in middle and high school, and/or in college will follow them into adulthood.

Once our children leave the college campus, they step into the real world and into the Sandbox. We want to know: Will they be prepared?

## Education in Preparation for the Workplace

What expectations should you have once you enter the workforce? What about for your sons and daughters or other family members? What is the law concerning sexual harassment in your state, and is the employer company or business obligated to protect its employees?

Imagine you are a young woman who just graduated from college, and you're working at a sizable company. As you expected, you're working long hours and doing your very best to impress your supervisors with your work product. A few months into your new job, you are invited to accompany one of your superiors on a work trip out of town. You have been selected from a pool of associates and are thrilled, especially because you believe your superior is showing confidence in you and your abilities.

You check into the hotel and find out your room is immediately adjacent to your superior's room. Was this placement intentional? What do you do? Ask the hotel clerk to move you to a different floor? Worse, what if you are not aware of this placement until, after the meetings, dinner, and drinks, you get to your room, only to discover that your rooms are adjacent? To make things worse, your superior invites you to his room to "review the results of the work meeting," and he is persistent and will not take no for an answer. Will you be able to detect his intentions? What if you say no despite his request? He is your superior and may have decision-making power over your career. How you respond may affect your future at the company.

If he is a stand-up guy, he probably wouldn't have asked you to join him in his room that late at night. Entering his room may mean you are at risk of being sexually assaulted, and it may be difficult to extract yourself without being harmed in some way. Believe it or not, this happened to a young woman we know as well. Her boss, a female, insisted she come to her suite after late-night dinner and drinks with a client, only to find out that her boss was looking for an intimate relationship. Our young female friend was not aware that her boss was gay.

At the very least, whether you enter the room or not, the incident will be upsetting, and you will be forced to reevaluate your relationship and your career at the company. This is a situation that you didn't bargain for and that you should be protected against by the company.

## What If Your Workplace Is the Entertainment Industry?

Singer/actress Alyssa Milano is credited with launching the #MeToo hashtag movement on social media when, in a tweet on October 15, 2017, she asked people to respond with "me too" if they had been sexually harassed or assaulted. "If all of the women who have been sexually harassed or assaulted wrote 'Me too' as a status, we might give people a sense of the magnitude of the problem."[18] The response on social media was overwhelming and resulted in millions of responses disclosing violators across all industries, including in Hollywood.[19]

The Hollywood #MeToo revelations struck a chord of shock and horror with the general public, causing a swell of support to shine light on a problem seriously affecting women since they first entered the workforce to this day. Before Hollywood, numerous sexual misconduct stories involving other businesses and industries made headlines for their egregiousness (Fox News, Fidelity, and Uber to name a few), but it was not until the famous movie producer Harvey Weinstein was accused by actress Ashley Judd—supported soon after by substantially similar allegations by Rose McGowen—that the swell of support became public outcry demanding real change. Famous actors and actresses have come forward with statements about how shocked they were by these news revelations, but for many of us, it's hard to believe they were clueless in light of all the other famous people who have admitted to purposefully overlooking the problem. People began to ask how it was possible that this type of predatory sexual behavior occurred and was permitted, let alone condoned and treated as an acceptable norm for decades in Hollywood.

Harvey Weinstein, arguably the most influential producer in Hollywood, was exposed for engaging in decades of sexual harassment against women, from employees, models, and hopeful actresses to well-known actors. Weinstein is known for his many Oscar-winning films, including *Pulp Fiction*, *Life Is Beautiful*, *Good Will Hunting*, and *The King's Speech*, and he is responsible for launching the careers of many famous actors and directors with his company, Miramax. When Weinstein's indiscretions hit the headlines, he had already reportedly settled at least eight claims over the years, including with actress Rose McGowen in 1997 and Ambra Battilana, an Italian model and aspiring actress, in 2015. (After he grabbed her breasts and reached under her skirt, she called the police.)[20]

Weinstein released a statement following the explosive news, which read in part: "I came of age in the '60s and '70s, when all of the rules about behavior and workplaces were different. That was the culture then. . . . I have since learned that is not an excuse . . . I appreciate the way I've behaved with colleagues in the past has caused a lot of pain, and I sincerely apologize for it." Since his statement, his list of accusers who have spoken publicly of varying degrees of sexual harassment and assault include more than eighty women, including actresses Angelina Jolie, Gwyneth Paltrow, Ashley Judd, Lucia Evans, Annabella Sciorra, and Daryl Hannah. It has become apparent that Hollywood knew of Weinstein's indiscretions for many years and did nothing, despite the tales of exposure in hotel rooms, explicit sexual requests in exchange for the promise of career opportunities, nudity, vulgarity, angry outbursts, and even violent behavior.

According to several recent articles published by Hollywood news outlets, Weinstein was mighty, a force of nature with influence well beyond imagination. You didn't cross him without the risk of physical harm or retaliation. He could make or break you. The commentary that ensued was scathing: "Weinstein didn't just exert physical power. He also employed legal and professional and economic power. He supposedly had every employee sign elaborate, binding nondisclosure agreements. He gave jobs to people who might otherwise work to bring him down, and gave gobs of money to other powerful people, who knows how much, but perhaps just enough to keep them from listening to ugly rumors that might circulate among young people, among less powerful people."[21] In another post, the author highlights that Weinstein's behavior was an "open secret" and "had been going on unchecked." She writes: "In an industry as stratified and competitive as Hollywood, when the victimizer has almost godlike power over careers, the factors that dissuade women elsewhere from reporting sexual violence are only magnified . . . In circumstances like these, it's the responsibility of the more powerful to fight on behalf of the weak. And the powerful dropped the ball."[22] Ashley Judd has filed a lawsuit against Harvey Weinstein for sexual harassment and defamatory statements that prevented her from receiving a role in the *The Lord of the Rings* movies. Judd claims Weinstein invited her to his hotel room and asked for a massage and to watch him shower. When she refused, he made negative comments about her to the movie director for *The Lord of Rings*, and she lost the opportunity.[23]

Weinstein is the perfect showcase of how power imbalance is key to sexual assault: a person in power imposing his will on another who cannot resist or defend herself for fear of retaliation concerning a job, opportunity, or reputation. The Weinstein Company, cofounded by Weinstein and his brother Bob Weinstein, is rumored to have tolerated (and even facilitated) forced liaisons with women, and so has found itself under investigation, with which, for the moment, it is cooperating. The board has since fired Weinstein and, on March 19, 2018, filed for Chapter 11 bankruptcy and released any Weinstein accusers from their nondisclosure agreements.[24] Divisions of the NYPD, the LAPD, and London's Metropolitan Police have opened investigations, and women continue to come forward[25] with allegations of sexual harassment and assault. According to reports, Weinstein surrendered himself March 25, 2018, to police in Manhattan, charged with first-degree rape and third-degree rape in one case from 2013 and with first-degree criminal sex act in another case from 2004. He has since been indicted.[26] He is expected to post $1 million bail, wear a monitoring device, and surrender his passport.[27] So it turned out that Weinstein, one of Hollywood's most powerful supporters of women's rights (he regularly gave to women's causes), is also a private champion of violating women, but in a ray of hope, Weinstein's legal troubles (more severe with each passing day) may do more for the women's movement than Weinstein ever did publicly.

We understand the uproar over Weinstein. His alleged actions went beyond sexual harassment to assault and rape, and his bad acts have been described as an extremely poorly kept secret in the industry. As more perpetrators are exposed, we are discovering other high-profile Hollywood figures have maintained similar reputations for years—and even decades—with industry insiders, secret only to the outside world. So why the seemingly sudden, explosive outcry when the news broke with Weinstein? JR and I scratched our heads. What about prior stories involving the entertainment industry with even bigger names, like Bill Cosby, Woody Allen, and R. Kelly? Their behavior is arguably even more disturbing. The reality is that this type of bad behavior may have been tolerated and permitted for many years, especially in Hollywood—such behavior often including sexual assault and rape. For example, does the "casting couch" sound familiar?

As a model or actress in a predominantly male-dominated decision-making environment, chances of success are low and opportunities fiercely competitive. Your fate depends on who you know, how you look and dress, and what you will agree to or tolerate (on the casting couch) in order to get a shot at fame. The casting-couch concept is not a surprise and has been in existence since the birth of the movie industry. It is the place where you are asked to relax while you are evaluated for your talent. The efforts to "relax" and "be evaluated" are then abused by perpetrators.

If you are a victim (or end up on the casting couch), you may have a choice on what to do if you are subject to sexual harassment. You can accept the terrible; defend yourself physically; report the behavior; or say "NO!" and walk (or run) away. For many women, however, the choice may not be easy or may not be available at all. Maybe, in the moment, you feel the only option is to comply, or otherwise risk your opportunity, your job, or, in some cases, your safety. If you complain (assuming there is a venue to which to complain), you may be labeled a troublemaker or blackballed and forever lose that specific opportunity or any future opportunity to work in the industry. We have all heard the obvious question, especially since the #MeToo movement launched: "Why wait all these years to come forward?" It is tough to understand and sympathize if you have never been in such a position. The simple answer may be fear. Fear of retaliation, fear of humiliation, fear of losing an opportunity, fear of losing a job, fear of not being believed, and fear of personal safety—and the violator takes full advantage of that fear.

So, if sexual harassment was known to occur specifically in Hollywood, what triggered the waterfall of women coming out of the shadows to finally tell their heartbreaking stories from decades ago? What triggered the explosive reaction and public outcry demanding change this time? For the purposes of this book, we will call this waterfall and reaction the *watershed moment*.

One theory is that the fear of not being believed was dampened by the strength in numbers of the voices coming out against a single violator. Sexual harassment and assault generally occur behind closed doors and out of view, making victims vulnerable to the classic "he said, she said" dilemma. A victim's account becomes more believable when the victim has corroborators who can verify what the victim shared at the time of the incident, evidence of the encounter (whether on social media or otherwise), and a description of the experience consistent with the present allegations against the accused. Journalists are more confident reporting such supported accounts, and companies are less likely to ignore the complaints. One person's experience may not be sufficient for the violator to suffer consequences. The more women and/or men who make allegations against the same person and who are perceived as giving credible descriptions of similar patterns of abuse, the more credible the accusations and believable the victims (as unfair as this sounds). With the launch and continuation of the #MeToo phenomenon, proof and conviction in a court of law no longer appear to be necessary to achieve real consequences to sexual harassment. The many directors and actors who have been exposed for their deviant behavior include Hollywood director James Toback, who's accused of incidents "in a hotel room, a movie trailer, a public park and meetings framed as interviews or auditions . . . typically to dry-hump them or masturbate in front of them, ejaculating into his pants or onto their bodies and then walk away. Meeting over."[28] The accounts are troubling, and the incidents, just like those involving Weinstein, were often coerced as a requirement to being considered for an opportunity. As of late last year, the number of women who have come forward against Toback exceeds two hundred, including actress Julianne Moore.

Anita Hill and others believe that credibility was lent because a celebrity complained: a woman "with status, fame, and succes commensurate" with Weinstein—namely, Ashley Judd.[29] As more and more famous women came forward with similar stories, their claims became more believable and paved the way for the average woman to stand up to be counted.

Some people disagree that a complainant's fame makes all of the difference. After Weinstein sexually harassed Daryl Hannah, she called "the powers that be and told them what happened," including her manager, the project's producer, and the director, Quentin Tarantino. According to Hannah, she experienced repercussions in response. Hannah told the *New Yorker*, "I think that it doesn't matter if you're a well-known actress, it doesn't matter if you're twenty or if you're forty, it doesn't matter if you report or if you don't, because we are not believed. [Us women] are more than not believed—we are berated and criticized and blamed."[30]

Maybe the watershed moment was caused by a combination of stature and strength in numbers. Ashley Judd's account was soon echoed by other famous women, including Angelina Jolie, Gwyneth Paltrow, Mira Sorvino, and others. Regardless, the vulnerability of women exists in almost every male-dominated industry, and sadly, it affects men as well.

It was disappointing to learn the sexual allegations about one of our favorite actors, Kevin Spacey, lead of the acclaimed Netflix show *House of Cards*. According to recent press coverage, in 1986, when Spacey was twenty-six, he attempted to forcefully rape then fourteen-year-old Anthony Rapp, today known for his role in the Broadway superhit *Rent*. Spacey has since apologized on Twitter, blaming alcohol for his actions, and is now facing a series of other allegations, including from employees who have been working recently with him on *House of Cards*.[31]

The consequences for Spacey have been devastating. Netflix has severed all ties with the actor, and his role in the blockbuster movie *All the Money in the World* was recast, costing production approximately $3 million to hire Spacey's replacement. In light of these events, the International Academy is not honoring Kevin Spacey with the 2017 International Emmy Founders Award. More men are coming forward, and Spacey is rumored to be receiving treatment for his behavior.

To make things worse, men are not the only perpetrators. Women in power can also be bullies, discriminatory, and sexist. Certain men and women in power have taken advantage of victims' vulnerability by forcing them to believe that succumbing to bullying, sexual harassment, and even assault or rape is the only way to beat the competition. We heard of one example where women seeking an acting role were asked by a woman to line up naked with only their private parts covered.

For Hollywood, accepting the invitation to a hotel room or a request for a sexual favor became an acceptable risk in order not to sacrifice the potential role or job. Acceptance became the norm.

In many cases, violators are bullies who feel empowered with license to objectify and abuse their victims for their personal gratification. They do not believe their behavior is inappropriate or wrong. Harvey Weinstein publicly justified his behavior by saying he grew up in the 1960s and 1970s, when, he believes, his behavior was common and acceptable.

For victims in Hollywood, remedies for sexual harassment have been limited. If you do not work for a company with fifteen or more employees, you may not have an HR department with which to file a complaint for sexual harassment. Since the #MeToo movement broke, the industry has implemented positive changes. On January 17, 2018, the Producers Guild of America adopted new guidelines designed to combat sexual harassment in the entertainment industry.[32] In addition, three hundred prominent female actors, agents, writers, directors, producers, and entertainment executives launched Time's Up, a multi-faceted initiative to combat sexual harassment, including the Time's Up Legal Defense fund administered by the National Women's Law Center to connect underrepresented female victims with attorneys (TimesUpNow.com) and the Commission on Sexual Harassment and Advancing Equality in the Workplace led by Anita Hill.[33] David Schwimmer (of the TV show *Friends*) and Sigal Avin (a director and screenwriter) have collaborated to make a series of short videos called *That's Harrassment* to illustrate different situations of sexual harassment. Versions of these videos will be shown on Fox, Showtime, CBS, Hulu, and Amazon.[34] These efforts are hugely important in affecting change, and we must remain vigilant and push to enact legislation that will discourage sexual harassment, bullying, and discrimination and will advance gender equality in the workplace. We will cover more on the topic of legislation later in this book.

While these efforts are underway, we must focus on how best to combat the prevalence of sexual harassment in male-dominated work environments. How can we positively influence how men and women interact and behave in the workplace, or Sandbox, of a company or organization for a more healthy and positive culture free of sexual harassment, bullying, and discrimination? How can we eliminate behavior that can negatively impact work culture, distract from pro-ductivity, and ultimately affect profitability? How do we learn to exer-cise civility, patience, and respect—that is, to *play nice* in the Sandbox?

# 3

# What to Do If You're Being Harassed in the Workplace

For many victims, filing an HR claim (assuming your company has an HR department or the ability to otherwise file a complaint) does not prove effective in stopping abuse or removing a perpetrator. The Weinstein Company, Uber, and 21st Century Fox are prime examples of businesses that allegedly looked the other way and did not enforce their own sexual harassment policies. Their priorities were arguably to safeguard the company's reputation and the presumed value of the alleged abuser to the company. The same is presumed to be true for some production companies in Hollywood: put up with the abuse to keep the actor or director in the public's good graces and to complete the project or movie in a timely fashion for release—all to avoid financial losses. The #MeToo movement has caused companies to take sexual harassment complaints more seriously, at least while sexual harassment is a "hot topic" in the media; however, we believe the current focus will not likely last. Filing a complaint with the company could take many months, risking continued exposure to sexual harassment, retaliation from colleagues who support the violator (if your complaint becomes public knowledge), potential harm to your career and reputation, and possibly forced departure from your company. In many cases, the drama of the process is too difficult and emotional to continue doing your job in any productive manner. You will need guts, patience, and emotional support to survive the process of filing a complaint.

## Start with Plan A

Before you consider going down this very difficult and tasking road of filing a complaint, we propose that you first deal with the violator directly. For the purposes of this book, we call this first approach Plan A. If, however, after you have implemented Plan A, you determine that the behavior is not being corrected and is intended to harm you, affects your productivity, and/or creates a hostile and offensive work environment, then move to Plan B—meaning, head to HR to file a written complaint. If the behavior involves physical violence, assault, battery, or rape (which are not covered under Plan A or Plan B), you should immediately file a charge with the police department. These are criminal offenses, and you should immediately report them to the local authorities.

Beginning with Plan A first, either on your own or with the help of colleagues, may help resolve the bad behavior without having to move to Plan B and file a complaint with HR. Explaining to the violator what behavior makes you uncomfortable and asking for such behavior to stop might be the best and most efficient course of action. Maintaining a calm and professional tone of voice with the violator is important. Your honesty might be appreciated. We have talked to several men who have told us that they would welcome more guidance on what acts are offensive and not appropriate. In some cases, bringing a colleague along who is supportive, or having a colleague (someone the violator respects) address the issue on your behalf, might also put a stop to repeat behavior.

# When Implementing Plan A, Be Aware of Different Personality Types

Plan A involves communication with the violator or a group of violators. The personality and intent of the violator or group of violators might complicate your communications. We agree with the theory that a sexual harasser generally falls within three main personality types: a predatory harasser (for our purposes in this book, we will call him "Tyrant Ivan"); a territorial, insecure harasser (we will call him "Insecure Trip"); and a dominant, egotistical harasser (we will call him "Ego Joe").[1] The following is a brief description of our view of these three personality types.

- **Tyrant Ivan:** The predatory harasser is a superior or a boss who holds the key to your promotion or increase in salary, creating a dilemma for the victim—resist and be punished, or submit and be exploited. The "motive . . . is a sexual conquest; harassment is the tool he uses to exercise power and compel an unwilling sexual partner to capitulate."[2]

- **Insecure Trip:** The territorial harasser is insecure and deliberately uses sexual harassment to protect his territory. For example, if a woman is perceived as a threat, he will "undermine her performance and eliminate her as a competitor . . . a way to fight dirty when a woman is too effective."[3]

- **Ego Joe:** The dominant harasser is looking to boost his ego and isn't necessarily looking for a sexual encounter. "When he harasses, he's a big man, he can compel a woman's attention (even against her will), he can intimidate, he can make a woman jump . . . he can feel personally powerful." Our favorite author on this subject, Martha J. Langelan, continues by saying that if he exercises this behavior in a group, "he can not only reaffirm his own masculine standing but uphold the status of the entire male group . . . a form of negative male bonding—building sexist male solidarity by exercising collective masculine power over women."[4]

Depending on the personality type and intent of the violator, your implementation of Plan A—your response to the sexual harassment—may be more challenging and the consequences more dire to your future career. Saying no to Tyrant Ivan may have far more serious consequences than objecting to behavior from Insecure Trip, Ego Joe, or a group of Ego Joes. As we move through the chapters of this book, we will, as necessary, refer to Tyrant Ivan, Insecure Trip, and Ego Joe to remind you of their personality types and to offer alternative suggestions regarding how to respond.

## Plan A: Steps of Communication

Once you have identified your offender's personality type, consider following the below steps of communication in dealing with the sexual harassment behavior.

- **Step 1:** Get the violator's attention. Stand up, establish distance, or motion for the violator to pay attention, and maintain eye contact.

- **Step 2:** Speak with a firm but calm voice. Aggressive language may put the violator on the defensive, and he will be thinking about how to respond rather than listening to you. Be calm, firm, and confident.

- **Step 3:** Ask the violator to stop his behavior. For example, if you are in a group of Ego Joes and they are making sexist comments about a woman, make yourself heard, and stop the male banter. "Gents, not cool. Please stop." If Insecure Trip keeps interrupting you during a meeting, say, "Please stop interrupting me." If Tyrant Ivan is touching you inappropriately, say, "Please stop touching me." If Tyrant Ivan is asking for sex in exchange for a promotion, raise, or other job related benefit, say, "Please stop asking for sex."

- **Step 4:** Give a quick reason for your objection to the behavior— tell him why you are objecting. For example, you are in a group of Ego Joes, and one of them says, "Can someone call Doris for some coffee? She has the hottest butt in town!" The other Ego Joes chime in with similar commentary. You might consider standing up and saying, "Gents, not cool. Please stop. That kind of language is not appropriate. You wouldn't want anyone talking about your daughter like that, would you?" If you get a response from an Ego Joe such as, "I would be proud that someone thought my daughter was hot!" engage him and say, "Are you sure? That kind of language about a woman is sexually degrading and insulting. Would your mom approve?"

    Let's look at another example. You are in a conference room at a meeting, and you are trying to make a point, but Insecure Trip keeps interrupting you. Turn your attention to Insecure Trip, and say, "Please stop interrupting me. You are welcome to offer any comments once I have motioned to you that I have finished making my point." Then continue to make your point. One more example: if Tyrant Ivan is touching you inappropriately, say, "Please stop touching me. You are making me uncomfortable. Please keep your distance, and don't touch me again." If Tyrant Ivan is asking for sex, say, "Please stop asking for sex. I am confident sex is not part of my job description, and I am happy to clarify with HR if you would like. Can we please get back to our work assignment?"

- **Step 5:** Repeat if appropriate, as necessary. If you encounter repeat behavior, remind the violator of your prior conversation. If you find that the violator or group of violators has questions regarding inappropriate interactions, take advantage of the opportunity to educate them. Make sure you are listening to their comments so you can respond appropriately. Try to engage them in the conversation rather than putting them on the defensive. You want them to listen, not be thinking about how to make you look bad.

As we have noted, if you determine that the behavior is not being corrected and is intended to harm, is affecting your productivity, or is creating a hostile or offensive work environment, you should then either express your complaint to the violator's boss (if you think the boss can put a stop to the behavior) or move to Plan B, below, and go to HR and file a complaint. If the behavior involves assault or rape (not covered by Plan A or Plan B), immediately report the offender to the police department.

Let's review a workplace example. Imagine you have a female colleague, Mary, and she starts attracting attention because of rumors that she is recently divorced and now available for dating. A superior (Tyrant Ivan) starts sending her emails, first asking her if she is "ready to date a real man" and then asking her out. He states he "can help her get over her ex if she goes out with" him. At first, she ignores his emails, but he is persistent. After several emails and her repeated rejections, he decides to request that she work on his team on a large new matter that will take months to conclude. Declining could be a career killer. He could claim that she is not a team player for refusing to work on the project. If she accepts, she is likely subjecting herself to continued sexual harassment. What should she do?

What makes her situation difficult is the fact that, as her superior, Tyrant Ivan has power over her career. Submit, or suffer negative consequences—the quid pro quo situation. If she works for a small company, her options are limited. If she works for a large company, she could request a transfer; however, a transfer in furtherance of her career may not be available. If a transfer is available, it may be risky if Tyrant Ivan is determined. He might take offense and decide to sabotage her future. If she discloses to HR the real reason for her desired transfer and confidentiality is not maintained, she runs the risk of retaliation (see Uber as an example[5]). In any case, it does not seem fair that she should be forced to pursue a transfer if she likes her job. Unfortunately, the exercise of any option could have potential negative consequences for her career.

Given her situation, if Mary has the courage, she should first try **Plan A** by finding his office and asking to talk to him in person. She should leave the door to his office open[6] and tell him as clearly and firmly as possible that she received his emails and is not interested in a personal relationship with anyone at work. She should communicate further that any such communications should stop because they're inappropriate and they make her uncomfortable. She should then emphasize she would like to work on his new project, since she is very qualified, but will need to decline if he insists on a personal relationship.

If Tyrant Ivan withdraws his invitation for her to work on the new project on her terms, she can thank him and leave his office. If you're in this scenario, make sure you take detailed notes of the date, time, place, and back-and-forth of any of your conversations, print all of his email communications and your responses, and note whether there were any witnesses and their identity. Make a senior colleague aware of the situation and of your visit with the violator in case he retaliates. The colleague may offer to talk to the violator on your behalf and resolve the situation for you. In certain situations, a conversation about the inappropriateness and potential consequences of the behavior can stop any further violation. If the violator chooses to continue with his bad behavior, move to **Plan B**, and consider filing a written complaint if possible. If you later file a written complaint with HR, the ability to provide evidence that you told the harasser his behavior was unwelcome and made another person (preferably at least one who is more senior) aware of the situation is helpful to support your claim.

Many other situations are less egregious, yet they often create similar emotional distress. Let's take an example involving a nonemployee violator situation. In one case, I was asked out by a senior member of a potential client's team for drinks "to get to know me better." It was late after meetings and dinner with a group of attorneys and clients. I had no interest in a personal relationship, and because he was a potential client, I had to *gently* express my concern that "getting to know me better" would be inappropriate and likely anger my superior. I told him that as a member of the firm, I was required to maintain a professional relationship with clients and vendors.

We were alone, and he kept pushing for a positive response, getting very close and rubbing my arm. "Your boss will never find out. We can keep this between us! It will be fun!" I knew his intentions were a problem, and I had to maintain my composure for the sake of the firm and the potential transaction we were pitching. I had to give myself the best chance of maintaining a respectful relationship and not lose the deal if I didn't play along with him. I mustered a *gentle* laugh and pushed him away, saying, "I am flattered, but I can't. We might be working together, and that will require a respectful relationship. How else will I be able to legitimately charge you legal fees?" I said it with a smile and walked away. Lucky for me, he seemed OK with my response. The client and I ended up working together on many transactions and established a good working relationship. He respected me as his company's counsel, and that was important to me and to my superiors at the law firm.

## Plan B: Filing a Formal Complaint

If the behavior does not stop despite repeated requests or after intervention by a colleague, or if the behavior is pervasive or severe, consider pursuing Plan B. Making the decision to file a formal complaint is difficult and might mean tough times ahead. Let's walk through an example of the likely process.

These days, companies with fifteen or more employees have sexual harassment policies and procedures in place, which they should be regularly updating and enforcing. Going back to Mary's situation (the woman who is recently divorced and gets uncomfortable emails from her superior), if the company provides for the ability to file a complaint, she must first decide whether the bad behavior rises to the level deserving a formal complaint. If the answer is yes, she will need to be fully prepared to provide proper evidence of the reasons for her claim. If you are Mary, document and date each instance of sexual harassment, and note if there were any witnesses. Ideally, do this on a personal laptop or in separate writing you keep at home to prevent the employer's ability to delete these notes from the company's network or company phone. Collect any physical evidence of harassment, including emails, photos, other objects (such as sexually suggestive gifts received unsolicited from the colleague), and any records from medical attention you required for harassment-related stress or illness. Print prior performance reviews for your records in case the harasser suddenly decides to give you a negative review in retaliation for reporting the harassment and/or abuse. Tell friends and coworkers about the violation at the time it occurs to establish corroboration of whether or not there are personal witnesses to the harassment. If witnesses or others have experienced similar treatment, ask them if they're willing to step forward and report what they witnessed or experienced in writing.

Once you (Mary) are comfortable with your evidence, seek support from a more senior colleague, especially if the incidents of sexual harassment are frequent. To that point: if you are a woman and work in a male-dominated environment with few or no other women, minimal or no HR department, and no policies and procedures regarding sexual harassment, finding support may not be possible. If that's the case, turn to colleagues who might be sympathetic, preferably those with a reputation for being fair. The person who hired you or another more senior person who has children or siblings of the same gender may understand your concerns and might help you walk through your complaint's potential consequences and reaction. In any case, finding senior support will help you be prepared and help provide encouragement, and you will find an ally who will be protective and encouraging. As we discussed in Mary's case, if this person works or socializes with the offender, he or she may be able to help you address or resolve the behavior under a **Plan A** approach directly with the offender, at a senior level, without the need for you to file the complaint.

If there is an HR department and you are inclined to give the violator one more chance, inform the department in writing that you intend to file a formal complaint. Use a detailed description of the basis[7] for your claim and your evidence, but request an informal, mediated discussion in an attempt to resolve the problem if escalation can, in fact, be prevented. If the complaint cannot be resolved within a reasonable and specified time with the alleged violator, however, proceed by filing a formal complaint. This gives HR a chance to resolve the matter without a complaint becoming "of record." Note, however, that notice of your intent to file a complaint may require the company to open an investigation. If the incident is egregious, however, consider moving forward with a formal complaint to protect yourself.

As the victim, consider what outcome you want. Do you want the abuser to be reprimanded and make a commitment to stop his behavior without any retaliation? Do you want to be transferred to another position without a pay cut or other retribution so you don't have to work with that person? Do you prefer being moved to a different floor so you don't have to interact with that person? If the harassment was severe, do you want compensation for lost earnings, emotional distress, and medical bills, and, if appropriate (i.e., the violator has shown a pattern of sexual harassment), do you want termination of the violator's employment? Making an internal complaint to HR (and thereby to the company) in writing, with copies as evidence, is critical if you ever want to hold the company liable for damages[8] concerning the abuser's actions. Success hinges on whether the company knew about the harassment and had an opportunity to remedy it, so make sure you keep a copy of everything you have documented and given to HR, just in case your complaint and any supporting information is "lost" by them during the process.

We recently heard a story about a woman who worked for a utility company that outfits large commercial projects. Her company's workforce is predominantly male, and she worked her way through the ranks over many years to a managerial position. When division bosses changed, her new—and much older—male boss did not treat her the same as her colleagues and was determined to prove she was not as capable as her male counterparts. Despite her efforts to convince him otherwise, he discredited her abilities, made demeaning comments about women, and behaved disrespectfully, including insisting she walk a dangerous construction project when she was a few months away from giving birth to her first child. She documented every disrespectful encounter and communication and included witness statements to corroborate her experiences. This was especially important in her case since she was a manager and the offender was a recent executive hire. The company had no choice but to believe her and take disciplinary action.

To make sure you are following the proper (and best) course of action with respect to Plan B, we strongly suggest you seek the advice of legal counsel. There are strict legal requirements and filing deadlines if you decide to pursue legal action against the company. These deadlines begin to run on the date of the harassment[9] (not of the complaint), and the EEOC requires that the charge be filed with the EEOC or other applicable state agency before you can file a lawsuit against your company in federal court.[10] The EEOC website has a list of organizations that can help you find an attorney to assist you if you need a place to start.[11]

You should also keep detailed notes of any communications with HR in case HR personnel fail to take action or in case they give advice or make comments that are contrary to the company's policies or local, state, or federal law. HR employees work for the company and may not feel comfortable proceeding against an alleged perpetrator who is also a senior executive to whom they may be reporting or who signs their paychecks. HR departments have been accused of being protective of the company and the alleged violator, especially where the violator is a senior executive or a contributor to the company's bottom-line profitability. Recent news stories involving Fox News and Uber are now fairly well-known examples.[12]

In the summer of 2016, the cofounder of Fox News and arguably one of the most influential executives in American television history, Roger Ailes, was forced to resign from Fox two weeks after Gretchen Carlson, former cohost of *Fox & Friends*, sued Ailes for sexual harassment. According to Carlson—a Stanford graduate and former Miss America—when she reported to Ailes that she was experiencing sexual harassment from a colleague, he called her a "man-hater" and told her just to learn to "get along with the boys." After she later refused to have sex with Ailes himself, she was removed as cohost of *Fox & Friends*, demoted to a show in a less popular time slot, and received a pay cut. In apparent further retaliation by Ailes, Carlson was later advised by Fox counsel that her contract for her new show, *The Real Story with Gretchen Carlson*, was not being renewed.[13]

The parent company of Fox News, 21st Century Fox, took action as soon as Carlson initiated her suit. The corporation hired a reputable law firm to conduct an internal investigation to look into Ailes's behavior and specifically to talk to Fox News's top on-air female talent. Their investigation discovered that Ailes's inappropriate behavior extended beyond Carlson to other female reporters, including Megyn Kelly. He would call women of interest into his office, ask them to close the door, and then make inappropriate sexual comments and attempt a physical relationship by touching or trying to kiss them. He was the boss, and a powerful man, and any attempt to reject his advances or file a complaint was a career risk—maybe even a career killer. After Carlson's firing and the filing of her lawsuit, more than twenty-five women came forward with similar harassment claims against Ailes, some of which go back five decades to his days as a young television producer. The claims portray him as routinely crude and inappropriate and as fostering a macho, insensitive culture at Fox. He preferred blonde women, and appearance was important—especially short skirts and long legs to draw viewers from the competition (like CNN). "Knowing how to play the game" was allegedly encouraged by Ailes for career advancement.[14]

After Megyn Kelly came forward to corroborate Carlson, 21st Century Fox had no choice but to remove Ailes. Carlson settled her lawsuit against 21st Century Fox for $20 million,[15] and although Ailes was eventually ousted, he was still paid a "separation/consultant package" of an unbelievable $40 million[16] to compensate him for his inconvenience—twice as much as was paid to Carlson, who had lost her career to Ailes first. It's not hard to see from the numbers Fox's alleged placement of value.

Nine months later, Fox News's most popular host and top asset, Bill O'Reilly of *The O'Reilly Factor*, was fired after a twenty-one-year run at Fox News, and—yes; wait for it—was paid up to $25 million in severance, equal to one year of his salary. The firing came on the heels of mounting pressure from advertisers who pulled their money after a *New York Times* investigation found that O'Reilly and 21st Century Fox had negotiated settlements of more than $13 million with five women who had complained of sexual harassment or other inappropriate behavior by O'Reilly.[17] To make matters worse, the *New York Times* reported just a few months later that a mere six months after the departure of Roger Ailes, O'Reilly had struck yet another settlement with longtime network analyst Lis Wiehl for a stunning $32 million, to be paid over time to maintain her silence. Despite 21st Century Fox's public commitment to changing the culture at Fox after the Ailes scandal, it turned out the company had decided to stand by O'Reilly and extend his contract for an additional four years for $25 million per year as one of the network's largest income generators.[18]

O'Reilly still denies any wrongdoing, claiming that in his forty-two years in the business, he never received a complaint from HR or the legal department. He claims further that after Ailes went down, a flood of women came forward, and the network had no choice but to settle the claims and fire him to prevent further loss to the company and to protect his family. Publicly known harassment settlements involving O'Reilly now total about $45 million.[19] O'Reilly expressed his anger about the developments on *CBS This Morning* when he appeared on the show to promote his new children's book, *Give Please a Chance.* When the roundtable of female colleagues brought up Megyn Kelly's book and the accusations involving Ailes, he responded, "I'm not interested in this." When asked to clarify ("Are you not interested in sexual harassment?"), O'Reilly responded, "I'm not interested in basically litigating something that is finished, that makes my network look bad. OK?"[20] His words and demeanor on the show appeared intimidating. On his eight o'clock show that evening, O'Reilly continued, "If somebody is paying you a wage, you owe that person or company allegiance. If you don't like what is happening in the workplace, go to human resources or leave! . . . And then take the action you need to take afterward, if you feel aggrieved. There are labor laws in this country. But don't run down the concern that supports you by trying to undermine it. Factor tip of the day: loyalty is good."

What do you think O'Reilly was trying to communicate? Be loyal to your employer at any cost because they pay you a wage? If you raise a concern about sexual harassment in the workplace, you're undermining the company and being disloyal? According to a recent report, 21st Century Fox has paid more than $85 million related to sexual harassment allegations since the Ailes debacle, with about three-fourths ($65 million) of that paid to the accused (O'Reilly and

Ailes) for their exit packages alone—essentially, they were paid to leave the network because of their illegal and inappropriate behavior.[21] This amount does not include the other settlements of roughly $13 million previously paid in connection with claims against O'Reilly, but even so, the disparate compensation between the victims and perpetrators is an outstanding example of a company appearing to reward terrible behavior and painting it as discipline.

Fox has publicly committed to taking active measures to change its perceived culture of fostering sexual harassment by hiring more women in top positions and as news anchors. To date, Fox has hired a new head of HR, and employees are now required to attend sensitivity training sessions. Female executives have been hired to head the finance and advertising departments since Fox's announcement of its intent to effect change, and Ailes's alleged "pantsuit ban" has been lifted.[22] In May, 2018, Fox News named former president of programing Suzanne Scott as its new CEO, making her the first woman to lead Fox News and Fox Business Network and the only female in charge of a major TV news organization. Scott has been with Fox News since its inception in 1996. Her promotion was criticized by some who said Scott was part of the team of senior executives who allegedly derailed employees' claims of sexual harassment under Roger Ailes and participated in retaliation against them.[23]

Let's get back to how best to deal with HR. Keep these three important goals in mind when speaking with HR: be honest, direct, and respectful. Maintain eye contact, and be assertive, with a calm, moderate, and cooperative tone of voice. Be confident and secure; avoid sarcasm and demeaning language. Be specific in describing the objectionable behavior, and avoid using words that might trigger a defensive or offensive response, such as "abusive," "rude," "sexist," or "racist." If you agree to meet with HR with the violator present, it is essential you be heard without encouraging the violator to react defensively and terminate the discussions. If you're interrupted, calmly and firmly request to be allowed to finish the description of the objection-able behavior. If possible, bring a witness with you. Whether or not the abuser attends this initial meeting with HR, once you're finished, ask that HR confirm that the described behavior is objectionable and vio-lative of company policy (assuming such behavior is verified through the company's investigation, if one is deemed necessary). Before con-cluding, remind HR that you will proceed with a formal complaint (if you have not already) if the behavior doesn't stop immediately.

You should practice the description of your account with a trusted advisor or mentor and ensure you have detailed notes to back up any incidents that are part of the complaint. Keep your notes as factual as possible, without emotion or opinion. Your notes may be entered into evidence to be read by a judge, and you want your account to be cred-ible. Ideally, hand HR a binder with the incidents of the objectionable behavior described by date in sufficient detail, including any pictures, emails, texts, relevant social media posts, or witness statements. The binder will lend credibility to your complaint.

If you decide to move forward with the claim, take the time to determine (with the help of your allies) if there's confidence that the company's HR department will take the complaint seriously. Will they enforce the policies and procedures of the company relating to the filing of the complaint, and, if so determined, will they implement any remedies and penalties against the violator, regardless of the stature of the perpetrator within the company? It will help your mental state to be prepared for all possible outcomes. Filing a formal complaint can be very stressful, and in many cases, the claim will not stay confidential. The process can also be very lengthy and take many months before any resolution is determined, risking continued bad behavior and retaliation by the offender or by other employees who may support the offender if the complaint becomes public.

Let's be realistic: even if the company does have an HR depart-ment and proper policies and procedures, there's no guarantee the company will take enforcement action, especially if the alleged violator is perceived to be of value to the company. There have been several recent cases in the news where HR was presumed to have not taken appropriate action or to have "looked the other way" because the perpetrator was a senior executive and "too important" to the company's bottom line. As a result, the affected employee suffered retaliation and was left with no choice but to leave the company and seek legal action (see our Uber and Fox News examples). If you decide to pursue a complaint and settlement with the company, know you may be subject to mandatory binding arbitration[24] to resolve the dispute, either as required by company policy or in your employment contract. The goal for most companies is to resolve disputes in a short time frame and to contain legal costs, not necessarily to look out for the best interest of *all* its employees.

In addition, for settlement purposes, many companies require confidentiality or nondisclosure provisions—particularly in discrimination and sexual harassment cases—to be signed as part of any written settlement agreement, allowing companies to maintain a shroud of secrecy over any allegations and protect their reputations and bottom lines. Mandatory arbitration and nondisclosure agreements also allow a company to contain the negotiation process. The company's management and lawyers are in control of the complaint process; employees are prevented from pursuing legal action through the public court process; and, ultimately, the violator is allowed to stay in his job. Consider Bill O'Reilly in the Fox News example.[25] He might have kept his position had it not been for the advertisers who started pulling their ads from the network (translating to millions of dollars in potential losses to the Fox News parent company and therefore incentivizing Fox to take action they otherwise proved reluctant to take).

In connection with any settlement negotiations, request that the company pay for independent outside legal counsel of your choice to represent you. The company may decline to pay for your representation since the matter is being handled internally. If you're unsatisfied with the company's handling of your complaint, you may then pursue a complaint at the federal, state, or local level, including with the EEOC under federal law (Title VII). As noted above, be aware of applicable deadlines and requirements for filing. Work with legal counsel to advise you on your rights and to assist with your complaint, whether at the company or later with any federal or state agency. Legal counsel should help you comply with proper procedures, requirements, and deadlines. If you're unable to afford counsel, check for locally available resources for assistance. The Time's Up Legal Defense Fund noted earlier in this book also lists valuable resources.[26] If one of the agencies finds your complaint is warranted, it will issue a "right to sue" letter that will then allow you to sue your employer under federal law in a court of applicable jurisdiction.

Going through the complaint process can be very difficult and emotionally draining. While the company is investigating your complaint, the violator may be continuing his behavior, or you may be suffering retaliation from the violator or his or her supporters. If you ultimately decide that leaving your job is the only option for your own personal health, consult with your legal counsel on how best to preserve a damage claim for lost wages and other monetary losses you might be experiencing.

What should you do if HR or the company executives who know about your complaint don't take action? In the case of Uber, Susan Fowler, the engineer who brought the company's sexual harassment problems to the forefront of the public, alleges that she suffered retaliation and that HR refused to take her complaints seriously. When she realized that she would not be supported and that her prospects for promotion were gone, she felt she had no choice but to leave her job—but not before detailing her experiences in an open letter to the public. Fowler's letter finally made the company pay attention and take action.[27] One option for Fowler might have been to send a letter to the board of directors at Uber, but would the company have then taken the same corrective measures? Whatever you decide to do, consult with legal counsel first to preserve your rights and to avoid any inconsistencies in case you decide to sue your company.

If you have a colleague who's pursuing a complaint, please take their situation seriously; they will need your support and encouragement to keep their job and your respect to keep their nerves.

# 4

# Why Women Are Afraid to Report Sexual Harassment

## Sexual Harassment Laws Are Complicated

The daunting and emotional process of filing a sexual harassment complaint can be sufficient to deter victims from pursuing any rights and remedies they may have. Understanding and following the requirements of the company's sexual harassment policies and the laws of your applicable jurisdiction can be complicated. If you decide to file a sexual harassment complaint with your employer or a claim with the EEOC (if the employer fails to take corrective action), consider seeking legal advice to understand the process and the timely filing of a proper sexual harassment complaint, in accordance with the employer's policies and the applicable laws, and to prepare for any requirement the company has for mandatory arbitration. Do this prior to signing any confidentiality and settlement agreements. This is especially important if you're not comfortable with how the company is handling your complaint internally. The complaint processes and procedures of a company are intended to protect the company, not necessarily the employee.

## Fear of Shame, Humiliation, and Intimidation

If you've been watching the flood of news resulting from the #MeToo movement, you may have noted that many sexual harassment claims remain unreported. Reasons for this include victims fearing they won't be believed and will face retaliation at work. According to the EEOC, three out of four incidents remain unreported, and of those ultimately reported, many are not even disclosed for years (or decades) until one victim finally finds the courage to report the harassment, causing others to follow suit. The #MeToo movement made en masse reporting possible with cases like Harvey Weinstein, film producer; Louis C.K., comedian; and James Toback, film director. We have fielded many questions from men (*and* women) on this topic, specifically about incidents that happened years and even decades ago.

In many instances, victims feel they have no choice. They fear that if they refuse, object, try to leave, or report the behavior, they will suffer embarrassment, humiliation, and/or retaliation; they won't be believed; they'll lose their job; or they may suffer (or exacerbate) physical harm. People in influential positions may be intimidating or known to be vindictive. Whether the violation is a slap on the behind, a lewd comment, a demand for sex, or even rape, a victim of harassment or assault may be reluctant to report what's happened to them for all the reasons listed above and more. A victim's fear of being shamed, not being believed, and/or retaliation is not an unnatural response to sexual abuse, even if it is sometimes difficult for others to understand.

You may be finding yourself wondering things like, "Why did she not say no? Why did she agree to have drinks with him? Why did she voluntarily walk into his hotel room on a trip out of town? Why did she trust that he would treat her right? When his intentions became clear, why did she not extract herself and get out of the room? Why did she allow herself to be placed in a vulnerable position? Basically, why didn't *she* do something?" This is called victim shaming. Here are some possibilities. Maybe the man was her boss or a colleague with influence, power, and credibility. If she had screamed, fought back, called 911, or shouted her story from the rooftops, would she be believed? He pressured her, exerted his power over her, and intimidated her into compliance. He may have invited her to his hotel room with false pretenses. He may have told her, "You know that I do not take no for an answer!" He may have had stature and power within the company and been valued as a significant contributor. If he denied the accusations, his side of the story would likely be believed over hers without damning physical or recorded evidence. She would have to suffer the shame of intense questioning and humiliation over what happened, and her reputation and career could have been ruined if she hadn't done the things that provided the opportunity for her assault. She may have felt she had no choice but to keep her mouth shut in order to save herself and her job, at great personal sacrifice, potentially with consequences affecting the rest of her life. Or maybe she was taken by surprise. It's difficult to keep your guard up all the time, and something innocuous, like a drink with a trusted colleague, may be or become dangerous in an entirely unanticipated way. For an actor, the stakes in Hollywood are high. If you refuse advances or complain about improper behavior, you risk being blackballed for the rest of your career. Many felt it was expected and part of the process of interviewing for an opportunity.[1]

Maybe you're wondering why this woman didn't just leave and find another job. But consider this: Why should the victim be required to find another place to work? What if she likes her job and would like to stay? What if her particular job is scarce? What if changing jobs would cause a loss of income or a cut in pay? Obviously, leaving would not be fair. It's wholly inappropriate to protect the perpetrator over the victim. In reality, many women do end up leaving their workplace because of fears about their future at the company or because they are being made uncomfortable, but the solution to the problem is not to displace and replace the victim.

Some may wonder: If she waited for years, maybe decades, to finally tell her story, why should we believe her now? What if she is lying to gain a few minutes of fame only to ruin the alleged perpetrator's career and even life?

For a moment, try putting yourself in her shoes. It is tough to disclose an embarrassing and humiliating incident that violated your person and affected you to your core for so long. Why would you voluntarily risk ridicule, harmful exposure, a ruined reputation, and your career, all for a few minutes of fame? What about exposing your family, friends, marriage, or children to the knowledge you were violated? Would you be willing for this information to be in the public domain? No argument, there have been situations where women have been untruthful, but reports indicate these instances are rare.[2] Victims are coming forward in an effort to finally bring the perpetrator to justice the only way they can—in the court of public opinion. They want to stop the perpetrator from harming others and to bring awareness to a problem that has been plaguing them for decades. Why should we believe these victims? For many of them, their stories in the media have included supporting evidence, such as corroborating accounts at the time of the incidents; similar patterns of behavior by the harasser experienced by other victims; prior settlements of similar sexual harassment claims; and other condemning disclosures. Victims finally have a more secure platform and the support to be courageous and share their experiences. This is a cleansing moment and a shocking awakening to a severe and widespread problem across all industries. Use recent news stories as discussion points with your colleagues, family members, and friends.

## Fear of Retaliation

In the context of work, if a complaint becomes public knowledge, the Sandbox can become unbearable for a victim, especially if the abuser is well respected or valued. It can start with exclusion from specific projects, meetings, and social circles. Then it can get more serious. Suddenly, a victim might be transferred to a less desirable division of the company, or they might face new, unfounded criticism of their job performance or poor attitude in order to validate any later retaliation against the victim, such as lack of promotion, cut in pay, or job loss. Retaliation can take many forms; essentially, it can entail any action that disadvantages the complainant or makes them feel uncomfortable or unwanted at work.

Until the complaint is processed and decided, the complainant will need support, especially from male colleagues when addressing a male abuser or, vice versa, female colleagues if the abuser is a female colleague. In many cases, it takes months to process a complaint, and victims may be required to continue working with the abuser, putting them in a tough position both mentally and physically. The situation will likely be a distraction to the company and affect the performance of its employees. The victim may ultimately find there is no choice but to leave due to lack of support and lack of a future at the company. Encouragement from senior colleagues who stand behind the complainant and speak up for them is critical to fueling the mental and physical strength a victim needs to get through the complaint process. Any retaliation that disadvantages the complainant violates the law and provides grounds for legal action.

# 5

# Introduction of the Playground Rules to Help Implement Plan A

## The Playground Rules and Sexual Harassment

Do you remember any "playground rules"? Whether you grew up with them or not, we believe many of those same rules (or guidelines or boundaries) can be applied today to the workplace's Sandbox to help men and women coexist and work together in a respectful, safe, and prosperous manner. Those very same rules most of us learned at a young age are helpful in stopping sexual harassment in its tracks. They are basic and should be familiar in concept, whether we first heard them on the playground, from our parents, or from a teacher or mentor.

Here are ten playground rules we believe are particularly applicable to sexual harassment:

1.  Respect the playground and its players.
2.  Treat others how you want to be treated.
3.  No bullying or intimidation allowed.
4.  Use nice words, be polite, and have good manners.
5.  Respect the boundaries of the players.

6. Work together to solve problems, using your words, not your hands.
7. Inappropriate treatment of players is strictly prohibited.
8. We share playground resources and take turns.
9. New players are welcome.
10. Do not jump off the seesaw without warning your playmate.

## Using the Playground Rules as Prompts

When you are implementing Plan A as described herein—or if you are having any general discussions about sexual harassment situations, with men or with other potential violators, bystanders, or even your children—use the playground rules listed above to explain why the objectionable behavior is inappropriate as sexual harassment—and what behavior might be appropriate. The idea is to use them as easy prompts or tools to remind your audience what type of behavior would not be appropriate or acceptable.

For example, for the group of Ego Joes who are making inappropriate comments, the following playground rules might apply: **#1. Respect the playground and its players.**

For Insecure Trip, who keeps interrupting you in meetings, the following rules might apply: **#1. Respect the playground and its players** and **#3. No bullying or intimidation allowed.**

For Tyrant Ivan, who touched you inappropriately or wants sex, the following rule applies: **#7. Inappropriate treatment of players is strictly prohibited.**

Reference the playground rules in your discussions to explain why the behavior is not appropriate. "Please don't interrupt me! Remember the rule you learned on the playground? 'Respect the playground and its players!'" If violators hear the rules often enough, they might remember them and associate them with inappropriate behavior.

# Putting Playground Rules to the Test: Real-World Examples to Illustrate How to Respond

If you are the affected employee, we want to arm you with tools to help you deal with uncomfortable situations without damaging your career in the process. As a bystander, if you are a coworker or a senior executive managing a workforce, we want to give you suggestions on diffusing and discouraging bad behavior and fostering confidence in your colleagues who are victims. If you are a parent, brother, or sister, we hope to spark improved awareness and better prepare you for dealing with these types of situations. You can only imagine the stories JR and I have to share. Below are some of those experiences and others, involving a myriad of industries, including real and current examples from many of our male and female colleagues, friends, and new professionals entering the workforce—as well as opinions from senior executives on how to respond, which may surprise you.

We hope these examples will help create a more healthy and prosperous work environment and career experience.

# Playground Rule #1: Respect the Playground and Its Players

## Scenario

You are called in to your superior's office to report on a matter, and he stops you midsentence and says, "Hold on. I can't concentrate right now. I am distracted by your boobs."

## Suggested Response

"Seriously? Did you really just say that out loud?" Motion to your chest, and say, "These may be attractive, but they are not yours to look at! Can we continue on a professional level without any further such comments? Remember the playground rule we first learned as children? 'Respect the playground and its players!' You should respect me as your colleague! If not, let me know when you can focus on the business at hand, and I will come back!" If this was a colleague, feel free to speak in a strong, firm voice. If he does it again, move to Plan B, and turn him in to HR. If this was a superior, don't be as aggressive. Be calm, focused, and professional in your address. If he does it again, move to Plan B, and report him to HR. When you see this person again, ask him if he understood your concerns and if you can move forward without any further such incidents.

## Scenario

You have been invited to attend a meeting with a client group scheduled for the next day, and your colleague asks you to wear a short skirt, "since that will be better for the meeting."

## Suggested Response

If a superior, say, "Sir, I don't think that is in my job description. Remember the playground rule we first learned as children? 'Respect the playground and its players!' You should respect me as your colleague! I will keep it professional, if that's OK with you." If a colleague, say, "I don't know, Insecure Trip, that might be a real distraction. Do you want me to also be bending over and picking up pencils too? Remember the playground rule we first learned as children? 'Respect the playground and its players!' You should respect me as your colleague! I would prefer to keep things professional, if that's OK with you."

## Scenario

You are on a conference call with clients and opposing counsel, and a heated debate ensues over deal terms. Opposing counsel starts laughing and says, "I feel like I am arguing with my wife!"

## Suggested Response

Laugh back, and calmly say, "I must take that as a compliment! Your wife sounds like a smart woman who will not back down! Remember the playground rule we first learned as children? 'Respect the playground and its players!' Let's be respectful of our working relationship, take a step back, and walk through the issues more calmly."

# Playground Rule #2: Treat Others How You Want to Be Treated

## Scenario

You walk into a client meeting that you have organized, and a male member of the client's team who has not met you and does not know you are the transaction leader says, "Hey, miss, can we get some coffee?"

## Suggested Response

"Hello, gentlemen, I am [state your name and your position]. Welcome to our meeting." Then look to the man who asked for coffee, and say, "I am happy to coordinate coffee for you." He will likely be embarrassed. If, by chance, you do not have an assistant or secretary to coordinate coffee for the meeting, have a coffee station ready prior to the meeting.

## Scenario

A male colleague keeps commenting on your body to other male colleagues, and a colleague comes and tells you.

## Suggested Response

Ideally, the colleague should defend you and say, "Hey, Ego Joe, that kind of talk is not respectful or appropriate and could get you in trouble with HR. Remember the playground rule we first learned as children? 'Treat others how you would like to be treated!' I am confident you would not want to be treated like that. Let's stop this behavior!" If he does not, go talk to the offender, and say, "Hey, Ego Joe. I heard that you keep talking about my body parts in public. Remember the playground rule we first learned as children? 'Treat others how you would like to be treated!' I am sure you would not want me doing that about you. It is not appropriate or respectful, so please stop. If not, I may have to go visit with HR."

---

### Scenario

A male colleague keeps commenting on another female colleague's body parts to other male colleagues in your presence.

### Suggested Response

"Hey, gentlemen, let's be respectful of Jenny and stop this kind of talk. It makes us all uncomfortable, and you are violating our sexual harassment policy rules. Remember the playground rule we first learned as children? 'Treat others how you would like to be treated!' I am confident you would not want to be treated like that. Let's not get you reported, OK?"

---

### Scenario

A man at a group meeting keeps winking at you.

### Suggested Response

Stop the meeting, and call him out. Say, "Excuse me, everyone." Turn to the offender, and say, "Insecure Trip, are you winking at me? Every time I look in your direction, you are winking at me! Remember the playground rule we first learned as children? 'Treat others how you would like to be treated!' I am confident you would not want me to be winking at you." Make sure you point at him. He will be so embarrassed, he will never do that again.

# Playground Rule #3: No Bullying or Intimidation Allowed

### Scenario

You are on a conference call, and the target client invites the group on the call to come visit in person to make a pitch. After the meeting, a colleague who's part of your team informs you that, despite the client's invitation, you will not be going, announcing, "Boys trip!" This same colleague has been saying degrading things about you to the boss and to your other colleagues.

### Suggested Response

Immediately respond, "Hey, Insecure Trip, wait a minute. I was invited, and I am going. This is a business opportunity, not a trip for boys to have fun! If you disagree, let's discuss with the boss, and I will let him know that you have also been talking about me behind my back. Remember the playground rule we first learned as children? 'No bullying or intimidation allowed!'" Stay calm, and measured and be polite. If he continues with his behavior, go see the boss, and, if necessary, move to Plan B, and visit with HR.

---

### Scenario

You are in a meeting with a group of guys, and you suggest a strategy on handling a certain problem. A guy in the group, who you know sees you as his competitor, keeps shuffling in his chair, rolling his eyes, and sighing out loud at what you have to say.

### Suggested Response

Notice that this guy is trying to throw you off your game and make you insecure about what you have to say. In this situation, it is OK to take a moment, look at him, and say, "Insecure Trip, I would really appreciate if you could stop your distracting behavior and allow the group to hear what I have to say. Once I am done, you can share your thoughts. Remember the playground rule we first learned as children? 'No bullying or intimidation allowed!'"

---

## Scenario

You are called in to your superior's office, and he indicates that to get a raise or promotion, you will have to show your loyalty by sleeping with him.

## Suggested Response

"Hey, Tyrant Ivan. I respect who you are and your reputation in the industry, but I want to earn my raise and promotions based on my work performance and with integrity. I need your help and counsel to do that without compromising our respective reputations. Will you please help me do that? Remember the playground rule we first learned as children? 'No bullying or intimidation allowed!'"

---

## Scenario

You find out from a colleague that you are not being invited to team meetings because your team leader does not like to work with women. You are the main contact for the client.

## Suggested Response

Call him out. Call another meeting, urgently, and include a person superior to the team leader. In the meeting, let everyone know that the purpose for the meetings is to get a strategy in place for the client and for the transaction the company has been tasked with closing. Show your expertise, and stand your ground. Show the group that you are in control. Intimidation and bullying are not appropriate!

# Playground Rule #4: Use Nice Words, Be Polite, and Have Good Manners

### Scenario

You are standing with a group of men in the hallway, and a female colleague walks by. One of the men can't help but comment on her long legs, big breasts, and tight skirt with lewd language, adding, "Oh, what I would do to her if I could!" The others in the group laugh at his comments.

### Suggested Response

"Hey, Ego Joe. Talk like that is not appropriate and violates company policy. Let's show some respect for our fellow colleagues. Remember the playground rule we first learned as children? 'Use nice words, be polite, and have good manners!' We would not want anyone talking about your daughters, girlfriends, or wives that way!"

---

### Scenario

Your colleague gets drunk at a company event, tells other colleagues that you are fun in bed, and makes other disparaging comments about your body. Another colleague who hears his comments tells you the next day.

### Suggested Response

Ideally, the second colleague should have pulled the drunk colleague aside and told him, "Hey, it is not appropriate to be disrespectful and talk about her like that. Use nice words, be polite, and have good manners. She will find out and may turn you into HR, which could get you fired!" If the second colleague did not speak up at the event, take him to the violator as your witness, tell the violator what you heard from the witness, and ask the violator to apologize to you and agree never to do that again. "Remember the playground rule we first learned as children? 'Use nice words, be polite, and have good manners!'" This is a very serious situation, and it will be very important that you be clear and firm, without any humor. We would recommend that you do not ask him to explain himself. He may get defensive and not hear what you have to say, especially if he was too drunk to remember what happened.

## Playground Rule #5: Respect the Boundaries of the Players

### Scenario
You are in a client's office for a meeting. Your client asks if you can arrange for your very attractive associate to have drinks with him after the meetings are over.

### Suggested Response
Be gentle with the client. Let him know that you do not have any authorization to offer up employees for personal visits with the client and that this type of behavior is not permitted by the company. Let him know that it would get him in trouble with her boyfriend and with the company! Remind him of the playground rule we first learned as children: "Respect the boundaries of the players!" He should respect the boundaries of the employees of the company.

---

### Scenario
You are at a lunch meeting with your colleagues, and a male colleague asks (either in private or in front of the group) if you are in a fun or wild relationship with someone and if you have sex in places other than the bedroom.

## Suggested Response

"Hey, Ego Joe, that kind of talk is personal and not appropriate, especially at work events, OK? Let's keep our conversations professional. Remember the playground rule we first learned as children: 'Respect the boundaries of the players!'"

---

## Scenario

You are at a client appreciation event, sitting in a box at a sports match. A client representative sitting next to you puts his hand on your leg and starts rubbing it, saying, "I am so glad we were introduced, and I hope we get to spend more time together going forward! Why don't we leave and have a drink in private?"

## Suggested Response

Move his hand gently. Smile at him, and say, "I look forward to working with you, too, but I am not interested in any personal relationship. I would get in trouble with the company, and I am already spoken for! Remember the playground rule we first learned as children: 'Respect the boundaries of the players!'" Remind him to respect the boundaries of the employees of the company.

Then get up and walk away. Make sure your boss knows what happened at the event.

# Playground Rule #6: Work Together to Solve Problems, Using Your Words, Not Your Hands

## Scenario

It is late at night, and you and a colleague are working on a deadline. Your colleague grabs your shoulders and starts rubbing them from behind as you are trying to revise a document you're both working on.

## Suggested Response

"Hey, Tyrant Ivan, no touching! Please back up, and respect my personal space!" Make sure you turn to him, look him in the eye, and say, "That is distracting and makes me uncomfortable, OK?" Remind him of the playground rules we first learned as children: "We work together to solve problems, using our words, not our hands! Respect the boundaries of the players!" Remind him that you are in a professional working relationship, not a personal one.

---

## Scenario

You are a female subordinate working on a project for your male superior, and you ask if he could take a few minutes to meet with you to discuss some issues that need resolution to finish the project. He tells you he is happy to help you if you swing by his place on your way home. It will be more comfortable for both of you, he says, and he will not take no for an answer.

## Suggested Response

"Tyrant Ivan, I would prefer to ask you these questions while at work. I promise it will only take a few minutes, and it would make me uncomfortable to come to your home. Besides, I need the resources in my office to complete the project." Remind him of the playground rules we first learned as children: "We work together to solve problems, using our words, not our hands! Respect the boundaries of the players!" Remind him that you are in a professional working relationship, not a personal one.

# Playground Rule #7: Inappropriate Treatment of Players Is Strictly Prohibited

## Scenario

You are updating a superior privately on a matter in his office, and he suddenly pulls you close and kisses you, with his tongue down your throat.

## Suggested Response

Push him away gently, and say, "I am your subordinate, and a personal relationship would not be appropriate. Let's keep things on a professional level. Thanks for understanding." Remind him of the playground rules we first learned as children: "Inappropriate treatment of players is strictly prohibited! Respect the boundaries of the players!"

## Scenario

You are at a company cocktail party, and one of your male colleagues (who is your superior and has had too much to drink) grabs you, pulls you onto his lap in front of others, and does not want to let you go.

## Suggested Response

Forcefully pull away, and tell him in a stern voice, "This is not appropriate. You are embarrassing yourself and me, and this is not funny! I don't want to have to report you to HR!" Remind him of the playground rules we first learned as children: "Inappropriate treatment of players is strictly prohibited! Respect the boundaries of the players!" Then, if you have witnesses, have one of them tell his boss what happened (or, if you feel comfortable, tell his boss yourself). This is a serious issue. His actions could be interpreted as representative of the company culture, and he may likely be a repeat offender.

## Scenario

You're the "newbie" of a group in your superior's office, and the superior grabs your behind while laughingly saying to the rest of the group that "you will have to get used to being grabbed when you are in my office."

## Suggested Response

Jump away from him, and say in a stern voice, "Tyrant Ivan, I don't think touching me is part of my job description. If you disagree, I am happy to clarify this with HR. Please do not do that again." Say it in a nice, but firm, manner so he gets the message. Remind him of the playground rules we first learned as children: "Inappropriate treatment of players is strictly prohibited! Respect the boundaries of the players!" If he does it again, move to Plan B and report him to HR.

---

## Scenario

A client openly flirts with you at an after-hours client event with colleagues and puts his hand on your leg. He tells you repeatedly that he wants to take you home.

## Suggested Response

Be honest about your feelings at that moment, but stay calm and professional since you are dealing with a customer or client of the company. Gently grab his hand, and move it away from you. Then say, "Your advances are making me uncomfortable, and accepting them is not part of my job description. Let's keep things professional." Remind him of the playground rule we first learned as children: "Inappropriate treatment of players is strictly prohibited!" Then get up and walk away. Make sure you tell your boss what happened, and ask him to please tell the client that his advances are not appropriate and that "going home with him" is not part of your job description.

## Scenario

You have been invited to a very important client dinner, and a colleague tells you just before the dinner that the only reason you were invited is to be "eye candy" to help close a deal.

## Suggested Response

"Insecure Trip, I am confident being 'eye candy' is not part of my job description. If you disagree, I am happy to confer with HR about your comments!" Remind him of the playground rules we first learned as children: "Inappropriate treatment of players is strictly prohibited! Respect the boundaries of the players!" Make sure you are well prepared for the dinner regarding the client and the deal you're trying to close. The group and your colleague will know that you are not just eye candy!

---

## Scenario

A male superior in a group meeting asks you several times to engage in tasks more appropriate for a staff person ("Be a dear and get coffee, organize food, make copies, fetch documents, etc. . . . Thanks, honey."), causing you to miss major portions of the meeting.

## Suggested Response

"Sir, we have staff on standby for this purpose." If you feel comfortable, remind him of the playground rules we first learned as children: "Inappropriate treatment of players is strictly prohibited! Respect the boundaries of the players!" Then go and make the call to that staff person. If you do not have staff folks to assist, arrange a coffee station in advance, or employ another person for assistance, such as the receptionist or file clerk.

## Scenario

A male superior in every group meeting asks you to take notes. You are the only female in the group.

## Suggested Response

"Sir, why don't we get Joe to take notes since he is the most junior member of the group and will learn a lot from learning to do that." If your superior refuses to honor your request, take the notes, but go talk to your superior about your concerns after the meeting. Remind him about this very important playground rule: "Inappropriate treatment of colleagues is strictly prohibited!"

---

## Scenario

Your boss just gave you a promotion that you have been hoping to receive for a very long time. At a later company event, he reminds you of this, and he asks you to reward him for getting you the promotion (and he does not mean lunch or dinner).

## Suggested Response

"Sir, I appreciate your support and the promotion. Hopefully, you believe I deserve it due to my hard work to date. What I think you're suggesting would be highly inappropriate and in violation of company policy, and I don't want to compromise our respective reputations." If you feel comfortable, tell him about this very important playground rule: "Inappropriate treatment of colleagues is strictly prohibited!" Stay calm and measured, and be polite. Then smile and walk away, saying, "Thanks for your confidence in me."

# Playground Rule #8: We Share Playground Resources and Take Turns

### Scenario

You are in interactive sessions with your male colleagues, and a colleague keeps belittling your comments.

### Suggested Response

"Insecure Trip, please be respectful and let me finish, and you can share your thoughts when it is your turn!" Remind him of the playground rules we first learned as children: "We share playground resources and take turns! Respect the boundaries of the players!"

---

### Scenario

You are in interactive sessions with your male colleagues, and your attempts to contribute are ignored.

### Suggested Response

Stand up and firmly say, "Insecure Trip, may I please speak?" Then contribute your thoughts without waiting for permission. Remind him of the playground rules we first learned as children: "We share playground resources and take turns! Respect the boundaries of the players!"

---

### Scenario

You find out from a male colleague that you are not receiving any "challenging" projects from your superior because you are a woman and "women are not able to work as hard as men and can't stay late due to household and childcare responsibilities."

95

### Suggested Response

Go visit with your superior. Let him know that you have heard his comments, and ask him to give you an opportunity to show him that you're very capable, efficient, and hardworking. If the project requires you to work after hours, advise your colleague that you are committed to your job and that you will stay the necessary hours (and will make accommodations, if you have children, or get the job done in a timely fashion from home). If he or she does not give you the opportunity, address your concerns with his or her superiors, or go to Plan B, and visit with HR. Remind them of the playground rules we first learned as children: "We share playground resources and take turns! Respect the boundaries of the players!"

## Playground Rule #9: New Players Are Welcome

### Scenario

A new female has joined your team. In a status meeting, as she is being introduced, a male colleague laughs and tells her that she will have to dress more provocatively to be a permanent member of the team.

### Suggested Response

A colleague could speak up and say, "Insecure Trip, you are no GQ, yet we have to listen to what you have to say, so leave Susie alone and make her feel welcome!" Remember the playground rule we first learned as children: "New players are welcome!" Susie could say, "Thanks for the suggestion. However, if I dress provocatively, you will all be distracted, and we will not get anything done! Remember the playground rule we first learned as children: 'New players are welcome!' You should be making me feel like part of the team!" Susie could also say, "I am happy to communicate your suggestion to HR and see what they say. I am confident they will not think you are making me feel welcome!"

## Scenario

You have been invited to a client meeting, and when you enter, a male colleague says, "This is Susan, our token female."

## Suggested Response

This is an opportunity for a male colleague to step up and be a leader. "Everybody, Susan may be the only female in the room, but she is someone you want on your team. She is hardworking, very smart, and will run circles around any guy in this room! Remember the playground rule we first learned as children: 'New players are welcome!' Please make her feel welcome!" If you are Susan, you can say, "I may be the only woman in this room, but I can certainly run circles around some of you, including you, Insecure Trip! Remember the playground rule we first learned as children: 'New players are welcome!' You should be making me feel welcome!" Think of cheesy sports talk: "I may be the only female in this room, but when we get to the one yard line, I am the one you need to get the deal over the goal line! You should be making me feel welcome!"

## Playground Rule #10: Do Not Jump off the Seesaw Without Warning Your Playmate

### Scenario

You're helping your boss with a pitch to a new client. Your boss can't make it at the last minute, and he sends you to make the pitch without him. The group is comprised of all men. As you are making the pitch (which includes a PowerPoint you worked very hard to compile), no one seems to be paying attention. Instead, they appear to be making lewd comments about your appearance and want to know when you will take them out on the town "so they can find out what is underneath your dress."

### Suggested Response

Ideally, your boss should have never allowed you to go alone. At minimum, he should have sent a colleague to go with you and sit in on the presentation. Maybe he did not care about the deal and was not worried about throwing you to the wolves. So, if you are left to your own devices, force the group to pay attention to you for a minute, whether by standing up and clapping your hands or by raising your voice and saying, "Gentlemen, my boss was not able to make this presentation, but I am very knowledgeable on the subject matter and helped prepare the power point. I would greatly appreciate it if I can go back and tell him that I made this presentation to you and you listened. I promise, it will only take fifteen minutes of your time, and I can answer any of your questions. If you help me, I will take you for drinks after, and the company will pay the tab. Does that work for you all?" You can always slip out of the bar after you pay for the first round of drinks. Your boss violated the playground rule "Do not jump off of the seesaw without warning your playmate." If you feel comfortable, remind him of this rule when you report back to him regarding the meeting—and hand him the bill for the drinks for reimbursement.

# 6

# Our Call to Companies: Promoting a Workplace Cultural Change

In light of the recent flood of #MeToo stories involving the prevalence of sexual harassment in the workplace, companies should review their internal policies and procedures and take affirmative action to "minimize the risk"—beyond the bare minimum of complying with state and federal laws. In fact, why not announce with clarity that your company is committed to eradicating sexual harassment and discrimination, that any violation will be investigated with vigor and without repercussions for those who report, and that those found responsible will suffer consequences, including possible termination? Mark Cuban, owner of the Dallas Mavericks, says he asked his HR director (Buddy Pittman) several times whether his organization had any problems with sexual harassment. Many other owners and heads of companies surely asked the same question when the #MeToo movement launched. However, as Cuban found out, simply asking the question wasn't sufficient. As it turned out, the Dallas Mavericks suffered from a pervasive sexual harassment problem that had not been contained even after Pittman was hired to update the organization's sexual harassment policies, which was prior to Cuban's ownership. Cuban says he was unaware of the problem.[1]

As the owner or head of a company, learn more about the process for determining whether there is a sexual harassment problem. When was the last time the company did an anonymous culture survey? What were the results? If issues were identified, how were they handled? Were policies and procedures updated to address the identified issues going forward? Did the company identify offenders and take action? If the company conducted regular culture surveys and implemented regular quarterly or semiannual sexual harassment and discrimination training for all staff and executives, would behavior improve? Would the work culture change for the better and, with that, the profitability of the company? What if the company also tightened its policies and procedures and provided incentives for reporting, compliance, and enforcement? What about real support and encouragement for victims, hiring more women in leadership positions to improve the male-dominated culture, and implementing better controls to establish equal status in worth and pay? If a company's work culture can be changed with swift and meaningful action, morale and employee performance are likely to improve and, eventually, positively impact the prosperity and profitability of the company.

## Taking Action Adds Value to Companies and Improves the Bottom Line

Are you paying attention to the bottom-line profitability of your company? There are only a few studies that review the impact sexual harassment can have on its employees, including tardiness, absenteeism, low productivity, low morale, staff turnover, and health-related issues such as stress, depression, and anxiety. One of the few available studies on the topic is dated as far back as 1988 and involved personnel, HR directors, and equal-opportunity offices representing over 3.3 million employees and 160 companies. The study concluded that "a typical Fortune 500 company with 23,750 employees lost $6.7 million a year because of absenteeism, low productivity, and staff turnover."[2] Other damaging effects of sexual harassment likely to impact the financial security of a business include costs to mental and physical health, legal costs and settlements, loss of reputation caused by the rise of transparency in the information age of social media and digital news outlets, and investor and financing losses. These effects, however, do not even consider the economic, career, and long-term mental-health consequences victims experience once they leave their job, either due to intolerable sexual harassment or due to how the company mishandled a harassment claim.[3]

Even when companies have faced high financial costs due to destroyed reputations and extremely expensive settlements for sexual harassment claims, companies are slow to change their perceived culture of sexual harassment until they are forced to take action, whether publicly or financially. See Uber and Fox News as examples. The reason is simple: companies are focused on current profitability and retaining high-contributing performers. In many cases, they "look the other way" and tolerate the behavior to preserve the alleged perpetrator's perceived value to the company. When the company is faced with "handling the problem" (the accuser and her complaint), the company settles for a remarkable dollar amount in exchange for the accuser's agreement to depart and maintain her silence with a nondisclosure or confidentiality agreement. Problem solved, and the high costs of potential litigation and damaged reputations for the company, the perpetrator, and the accuser have been avoided. Hopefully, the company has sufficient sexual harassment insurance. In the past seven years alone, US companies have paid out more than $295 million in public penalties over sexual harassment claims.[4] Consider a January 2016 ruling in which a Los Angeles jury awarded a female lawyer, Minakshi Jafa-Bodden, $924,500 in compensatory damages and $6.4 million in punitive damages for harassment by yoga guru Bikram Choudhury.[5] This does not even include private settlements given in exchange for nondisclosure agreements. Even more disturbing is the fact that many of the settlements allowed the abusers to stay in their positions; if they were fired, they were still able to further their careers in new positions at other companies (potentially risking a continuation of their bad behavior).[6] Companies are not focused on the long-term financial impact of sexual harassment, which results from a deterioration of workplace culture, costs associated with the mental and physical health of its employees, financial costs relating to employee turnover, and reputational losses. Uber lost customers to its competitor Lyft, and, based on a recent article, "with the ever-increasing sexual harassment complaints and the #deleteuber campaign, the company saw a loss of $703 million and a consequent exit of its CFO."[7] Following Fowler's post about how she was treated at Uber, two women engineers filed lawsuits against Uber in California in October, 2018, alleging gender and race discrimination regarding unequal pay and promotion. This class action has now been settled for $10 million and is intended to include compensation for sexual harassment claims.[8]

Fox News started losing advertisers during the Bill O'Reilly debacle and reportedly spent more than $110 million on matters related to sexual harassment within a nine-month period.[9] We believe that's ultimately why Fox fired Bill O'Reilly. Were the noted losses enough to cause Uber and Fox News to take real action to change their alleged toxic culture of sexual harassment? Losing customers and advertisers and paying large settlements was undoubtedly going to have a financial impact.

Even when the company does the right thing by firing a highly profitable, popular, or valuable offender, replacement costs can be staggering. The recent movie *All the Money in the World* was originally due for release at the end of 2017, but it was put on hold to reshoot all the scenes that included Kevin Spacey (who was fired following accusations of sexual misconduct, assault, and harassment of men). Spacey was replaced with Christopher Plummer, and the expense of completing the movie supposedly exceeded $10 million.[10]

There are many other financial risks to companies, including those resulting from damage to reputations, such as difficulty in recruiting, withdrawal of investors, sponsors, and vendors, and loss of financing by banks and other traditional resources. Who wants to partner with or invest in a company that has a culture that potentially breeds conflict and lawsuits? A recent example involves the CEO of CBS, Leslie Moonves, arguably one of the most powerful media executives in America and a vocal supporter of the #MeToo movement. Shares in CBS fell more than 6 percent (approximately $1.4 billion in market value, according to *Variety*) after accusations surfaced in the *New Yorker* that he'd committed several incidents of sexual harassment dating back several decades.[11]

One single sexual harassment claim could financially ruin a small or family-run business due to legal fees, settlement fees, and the loss of future business. Even if a company has sufficient insurance coverage, it might not repair the damage to employee morale or the public's perception of the company. Failing to take action will very likely have severe ramifications. Tolerating a culture of bad behavior perpetuates a hostile working environment and generally causes a decline in the company's reputation. Deteriorating morale, health, and productivity, loss of talented employees, clients, and customers, increases in litigation and insurance expenses, and loss of investors will ultimately affect a company's financial health and potentially risk the company's future.

## Collaboration of Men and Women Can Increase Profitability

Plenty of recent studies and reports underscore the importance of gender diversity in leadership positions of the Sandbox.[12] A greater number of women in senior leadership and management positions was tied with better performance in organizations, including better financial performance, higher retention, better reputation, better problem solving, and less conflict.[13] The leadership qualities exercised by women are critical to a company's success. Women are more likely to be better at overall organization and details, including developing, managing, and motivating teams, encouraging participation, communicating changes in direction, setting expectations, and assessing capabilities. Women are more likely to be emotionally connected and able to motivate and inspire.[14]

We believe that men and women working together can be valuable assets to one another, especially in a company environment. The variety of viewpoints, market insights, and ideas that arise when we collaborate with people of different genders, ethnicities, religions, races, and sexual orientations results in improved problem solving and profitability. If you need proof, a Gallup study involving eight hundred business units from two companies in the retail and hospitality industries found "that hiring a demographically diverse workforce can improve a company's financial performance."[15] Diverse teams are also more likely to challenge one another's ideas, assumptions, and potential biases, to reexamine facts, and to exercise greater scrutiny—allowing the team to be more objective, competitive, and innovative. A diverse team is less likely to make mistakes.[16] As David Rock and Heidi Grant note, "Hiring individuals who do not look, talk, or think like you can allow you to dodge the costly pitfalls of conformity, which discourages innovative thinking."

In a male-dominated environment, being a woman can have enormous advantages. Women can be a gentle and calming influence. In difficult negotiations, a woman's firm but gentle voice and friendly female gestures are less threatening, and women are typically better team players, more concerned with relationships and mutual best interest than intimidation.[17] We agree with Lisa Gates in her article for *Forbes*: "[Women] are much more naturally disposed than men to produce collaborative, durable agreements—meaning our agreements last, and don't induce lingering resentment. . . . The only thing we lack is confidence and a bit of study in the exquisite tools and strategies of . . . negotiation."[18]

However, temperament is not sufficient. My father used to tell me that if you work for a difficult superior or client, find a way to add value and earn that person's trust and respect. "Work hard to become an expert." "Knowledge is power." Learn how to "make your boss look good in the eyes of others," as opposed to demeaning his or her intellect. That last one was especially important for JR and myself in our respective professions. Never correct your boss or client or make that person look bad in front of others. The foregoing applies to female clients and bosses as well. It's even better if you can "manipulate that person into thinking the idea was his or hers." A few of my father's famous words. JR calls it "stroking" the client or boss, or "working JR's magic." No man wants a female to "boss him around" or "correct his opinion on a matter." Interestingly, men can do that to other men all day long and don't appear offended. JR and I are known as calm, level-headed negotiators who can make difficult parties compromise with tact and patience. We both learned how to add value and complement the strengths and weaknesses of our counterparts. We learned how to modify behavior and engender respect for ourselves and the female members of our teams. We both became successful in our professions and became preferred hires—especially by our male clients.

Let's get back to the financial impact of sexual harassment. In light of the potential financial consequences to a company or organization, why is creating a work culture free of sexual harassment not a priority? Why are we not populating the Sandbox with more women in leadership positions to help eradicate such cultures and potentially increase profitability? More action by companies must be taken to increase gender diversity within its workforces and in leadership. In 2010, the "30% Club" was launched as a campaign in the United Kingdom, with the goal of achieving 30 percent women on FTSE-100 boards by 2020. Since its launch, the number of female directors has grown from 12.5 percent to 27.9 percent; however, companies' response to commit to the pledge has been slow—only fourteen CEOs of the UK's largest one hundred publicly traded companies have made the pledge.[19] The reason for lack of promotion of women to leadership positions may not necessarily be issues with the women's qualifications; rather, it may be cultural beliefs and implicit biases[20]—such as a belief that women are weak and not able to lead effectively, or women of a certain body type cannot be successful, or women are not confident enough to ask for a promotion.[21] These beliefs and biases may have a severe negative impact on the development of women and the overall recognition of women as capable leaders. In March 2015, the German parliament passed a new law requiring a thirty percent quota of women to be appointed to the nonexecutive supervisory boards of the country's largest companies and senior leadership positions in the public sector.[22] Other countries, including Norway, France, the Netherlands, and Italy, already have corporate gender quotas in place. In Germany, companies have been slow to comply. The legislation does not appear to have penalties for noncompliance, and companies claim a lack of properly trained women for these positions.[23] Nonetheless, this type of legislation could be helpful in the United States.

## Unintended Consequences of the #MeToo Movement: Don't Make Excuses

Let's be clear. Currently, men outnumber women in leadership positions at most companies. This is reality. Until this changes, if women are to prosper and be promoted in the workplace, the guidance, support, and mentorship of men will be important to their success. Why, you ask? Men can help women understand how to conduct business in a male-dominated environment, how to communicate with men, and how to make them listen. Men have relationships with other men and connections that are important in fostering business. Men can help women make it to the top in a business world dominated by men and can be valuable allies. Now, with the #MeToo movement, and with many men in almost every industry having been fired or had their careers destroyed, there is growing concern among men about sexual harassment and what behavior might get them in trouble. Going forward, men say, they are going to be cautious and stay away from any activities with women in the work environment. Men, how about you be educated instead and learn what behavior is not appropriate so we can avoid sexual harassment going forward?

We can say without hesitation that men have nothing to worry about if their motives are honorable. If you are engaging with any woman, in a work-related context or not, with an ulterior motive of sexual gratification, then don't meet with her. It's that simple. You can have lunch with a colleague in a public restaurant, meet with any woman behind closed doors, and have a drink with her after work at a bar as long as your motives aren't sexual and you are not making her uncomfortable. You can also work together on a project after hours and travel with a woman out of town. If you are worried about perception and gossip, then meet in public places and during the day. However, if you are a stand-up guy with nonsexual motives, you have nothing to worry about. Just don't plan meetings in suspect places. Women do not want to lose important business relationships and mentoring friendships with men, and discrimination against women is not the solution to sexual harassment.[24]

Until women populate an equal number of leadership positions as men, women may want the advice, guidance, and mentorship of men to help further their careers. Women are not asking for men to stop interacting with them. That is not the purpose of the #MeToo movement. The #MeToo movement started as a hashtag and spread virally on social media to help demonstrate the widespread prevalence of sexual harassment and assault, especially in the workplace. The pervasive problem underscores the urgent need to strengthen legal protections, to transform toxic, misogynistic male-dominated cultures in the workplace, and to promote transparency in how businesses handle sexual harassment complaints and punish abusers. Transparency and changing workplace culture are critical priorities for more positive, healthier work environments. Promoting and maintaining healthy relationships between men and women in the Sandbox is likely to improve productivity and retention of women in the workforce—for a more prosperous work environment.

## Consider the Following Immediate Action Items

1.  Implement and regularly update policies and procedures against sexual harassment, bullying, discrimination, and retaliation for reporting in compliance with applicable laws (including procedures for reporting, investigating, and disciplinary action), and encourage employee feedback.

2. Conduct anonymous employee surveys to get a clear assessment of the company's culture and work environment and the effectiveness of the company's sexual harassment policies and procedures. If necessary, hire an outside, independent expert to help identify and determine whether there is a need for new policies or for revisions to old policies and procedures.

3. Company policies should include mandatory codes of conduct and organizational values.

4. Set a tone of "zero tolerance" for even the highest, most respected level of employee (such as the CEO). Make it clear the company will maintain and enforce, without exception, a zero-tolerance policy for sexual harassment. The CEO should frequently remind employees of this policy (including codes of conduct and organizational values), verbally and with regular memos, in the sternest and most forceful tone possible. Make sure that your chosen person is not known or rumored to be a perpetrator himself or herself.

5. The board and HR should study any past settlements or current, ongoing cases at the company related to sexual harassment or discrimination to understand the behavior, the potential for recurrence, how the incident was reported and handled by HR and by the company, and how the matter was resolved with the victim and the perpetrator. Determine any corrective action needed, then make corrections promptly.

6. Hire an outside consultant and appropriately trained HR employees who are current on the topics of sexual harassment, bullying, and discrimination.

7. HR and/or a consultant should conduct mandatory training for staff and executives at least twice a year. Include specific training involving bystanders and the concept of implicit bias.

8. Training should consist of an interactive session on unwelcome sexual advances (whether verbal or physical) and appropriate conduct that does not constitute sexual harassment (such as providing praise).

9. Policies and procedures should provide a complaint process that is clear and easy to follow. They should also provide assurances that any complainant or participant in the process will be protected against retaliation, that confidentiality will be protected as best as possible, that the investigation will be conducted on an impartial basis, and that the company will take immediate and appropriate corrective action if the review determines that harassment has occurred, including discipline or termination (no matter how senior or how valuable the violator may be to the company).

10. Provide a link on the company's website available to all employees and executives regarding the company's zero tolerance for sexual harassment, bullying, and discrimination. Include sublinks to the policies, to the procedures for filing a claim, to enforcement and corrective actions, and to a reminder regarding upcoming mandatory training sessions.

11. Employees should be advised that they have the right to bypass HR and complain directly to a board member or any senior executive designated by the company for such purposes.

12. Institute an anonymous complaint system (or other "safe" mechanism for reporting) for employees who wish to complain anonymously. Any anonymous complaints should be provided to HR and the board of directors (or a subcommittee of the board designated for such purposes).

13. Hire an outside HR consultant and legal counsel to handle complaints against executive employees, and allow victims to report directly to such consultants to reduce fear of retaliation.

14. Supervisors and managers should be required to immediately report suspected sexual misconduct (or face discipline for failing to report the same). HR should be required to regularly report directly to the board (or a subcommittee designated for such purposes) regarding any sexual harassment complaints, regardless of how frivolous the claim might be. This is to affirm HR's role as an advocate not only for employees but also for the company, removing pressure on HR to protect senior executives over the employees.

15. Employees should be encouraged and supported in regard to proper reporting and enforcement, including bystanders who intervene or report bad behavior. Additionally, failing to report bad behavior or allowing the bad behavior to happen should be discouraged and cause disadvantage. This will go a long way to showing victims the support of their management, supervisors, and peers.

16. The board and executives should be fully aware of current policies and procedures and be fully supportive of the consequences for violations, no matter how senior or valuable the violator is to the company.

17. Take all complaints seriously. Investigate as thoroughly and as impartially as possible, with compassion and professionalism. Maintain detailed notes; take formal statements from all known witnesses; and obtain copies of any inappropriate emails, texts, letters, and other communications, including photos and videos. Leave no stone unturned. Upon completing your investigations, prepare a complete report with recommendations regarding the outcome of the investigation. Know that this may end up as part of a court proceeding. Consider establishing a committee with members from across the company tasked solely with processing and directing the investigation of any complaints (to help lend credibility and confidence to the process).

18. Take immediate and appropriate corrective action when it is determined that harassment has occurred. Penalties for violation should be rigorously and consistently enforced. Consider putting the accused on a paid leave of absence during the investigation. If exonerated, he or she should be reinstated. If the employee is found responsible and the behavior warrants termination, the employee should be terminated regardless of seniority and without the payment of any indemnity or severance package. Other disciplinary actions might include mandatory training, counseling, reductions in compensation or loss of bonuses, demotion, removal from leadership positions, and transfer to another location.

19. If the violator is found responsible, generously support the recovery of the abused, such as by supporting counseling services, transfer to a new division or floor, and reimbursement of legal or medical expenses. Provide regular positive encouragement, and promptly punish any retaliatory behavior.

20. Any settlements agreed to by the company should not be conditioned upon confidentiality or a nondisclosure agreement. The complainant should have a right to confidentiality if requested.

21. Any settlement negotiations, including mediations or arbitrations, should be conducted by an independent third party not affiliated with the company.

22. Any settlement negotiations involving an executive of the company or involving egregious behavior should be performed with counsel for the victim, chosen by the victim and reimbursed by the company.

23. Any new hires—specifically executives—should be vigorously vetted for any history of sexual harassment incidents or rumors (and

the company's policies against sexual harassment should prohibit any such employment). For example, a recent article published in the *Wall Street Journal* highlights how rainmakers accused of sexual harassment can change jobs with ease.[25] In one case involving Mayer Brown's New York office, flowers arrived a few days after a new hire with a hefty book of business did. The card read, "Thanks for taking him." Signed: "The women."[26]

24. New hires should receive entry training on the company's zero-tolerance policies and enforcement, including immediate termination, regarding sexual harassment, bullying, and discrimination.

25. Senior executive employment contracts should require strict adherence to company policies and procedures regarding standards of conduct, sexual harassment, and consequences for violation, including the right to prompt termination with cause, without indemnification or severance payments.

26. Set gender diversity inclusivity goals for upper management, and hold management accountable for compliance.

27. Hold men and women in leadership positions accountable for supporting a safe and fair workplace for women (and men) and for using the power of their positions to call out and modify lousy behavior of perpetrators, thus helping to change the culture of the company.

28. Develop hiring strategies that increase gender diversity without reducing or ignoring merit. Consider a quota percentage of women. See prior discussion involving quotas of 30 percent in other countries.

29. Promote qualified women and minorities to leadership positions, and require every search committee seeking executives,

including for the position of CEO, to include qualified women and minorities.

30. Promote qualified women and minority representation on boards, panels, and leadership teams, including at client events, client pitches, and speaking engagements.

31. Share gender pay comparisons with other companies.

32. Provide proper mentorship and sponsorship opportunities for women and leadership training to allow women the chance to succeed within the company and achieve leadership and executive positions.

The #MeToo movement began with an explosive firestorm and is likely to continue. No company or business should take this time for granted. If there are any problems at your company, you can be certain they will surface. Be proactive; focus on the possible negative impact of a culture laden with sexual harassment, bullying, and discrimination; and take appropriate action. If we can make sexual harassment training and proper behavior a priority, we can raise awareness, encourage better behavior, and lessen the instances of sexual harassment and its impact on work productivity. There are plenty of resources to consider on this topic,[27] and today, many law firms have departments and experts that can assist with company endeavors regarding sexual harassment.

A company that fosters a healthy environment and culture in which men and women diverse in race, ethnicity, and sexual orientation work together with civility and respect, is likely to achieve greater success and financial prosperity. Let's get to work cleaning up the Sandbox to achieve this goal for future generations.

# Other Playground Rules Applicable to Companies and Important for Company Employees

There are a few playground rules that are applicable to company employees and that colleagues should remember in their daily interactions.

A real playground might have a rule that says "Enter at Your Own Risk" to protect against liability for equipment that's flawed or broken. If you get hurt on the playground, the injury is at your own risk, and it's understood that you must be cautious and enter at your own risk. How does this rule apply to the work environment? What if you're a woman and you walk into a conference room with all men? Should you have to enter the room with caution and at your own risk? Many women would advise you to do just that. Prepare yourself to be subjected to some form of sexual harassment. Companies, however, are required by law to protect you from any such behavior (in this metaphor, broken equipment and potential injury). The applicable company playground rule is: "Care for your playground members—entering should not be at your own risk!"

Let's take an example.

### Scenario

A woman walks into a meeting and sees men hovering over a *Playboy* magazine, commenting on the centerfold's "tits" and "beehive," or perhaps the men are watching a video of animals mating. The men continue with their activity laughing and even invite her to take a look.

**COMPANY PLAYGROUND RULE #1**

Care For Your Playground Members— Entering Should Not Be at Your Own Risk

### Suggested Response

"Seriously, Ego Joes? I am not going to run to HR, but someone else watching you may get offended and do just that! Also, did you all not know that your computer activities are being monitored by the company?" In each case, remind them of the applicable company playground rule: "Care for your playground members—entering should not be at my own risk!" The *Playboy* magazine example actually happened to me, and the violators included a partner at the law firm. His back was to the door of his office, and I could see that he and the group were studying the centerfold—a spread-eagled naked woman. They were not deterred when I walked into the office. I immediately commented to the partner, "Ego Joe, if someone sees you, they might report you to HR. Aren't you supposed to be setting an example as a partner? Put that away before you get caught! There is a company playground rule that applies here: 'Care for your playground members—entering should not be at my own risk!'" My tone of voice was lighthearted and friendly, but I kept my admonishing posture over the group until they put away the magazine. The woman should not be exposed to behavior that makes her uncomfortable. This is an opportunity for a man in the room to exhibit leadership qualities and show that he "cares for the playground and its members." He should ask all of the men in the room to stop the objectionable behavior immediately now that the female colleague has entered the room. Another playground rule that applies to this situation: "Remind others of the rules; don't be a bystander!"

COMPANY
PLAYGROUND
RULE #2

Remind Others
of the Rules;
Don't Be a
Bystander

If a man does not step up to stop the behavior, the woman should ask the group to stop. "Gentlemen, what you are doing is not appropriate. Please stop, and let's get back to work!" The men should immediately obey.

If you work for a company, employees are likely subject to policies regarding sexual harassment. To promote a work culture free of sexual harassment, it is critically important to enforce these policies and protect those who are violated. If you walk by a desk and notice a group of men looking at something on a computer screen, making lewd remarks, and laughing, don't remain silent and continue on your journey, especially knowing that women are in the vicinity or are likely to walk past. The same goes for watercooler talk of the previous night's sexual conquests or nasty comments about women walking by. Speak out, and ask them to stop. Remind them that they're subject to the company's sexual harassment policies, and tell them you don't want them to get in trouble. Remind them of the company playground rule: "Care for your playground members!" Men will listen to men. We realize this may be more difficult if the violator is a superior. The male bystander may not speak out for fear of being ridiculed and bullied. If this is the case, distract the conversation from the topic of the sexual harassment, or pull the violator aside and talk to him privately. If you ask them to stop in a gentle but firm voice—maybe with a little humor—we believe they will listen. Be brave, and try it! Don't be a bystander.

Here is another example. If you're out of town, after client meetings, and you overhear a more senior colleague or a client asking a female associate to go to his hotel room to "review the day's events," don't stay silent. She's likely very uncomfortable. Let the colleague or client know that fraternizing with female employees is not permitted. Your input will likely discourage repeat behavior. Don't be a bystander.

Another example. You are at happy hour with the guys, and a female colleague leaves the table to go to the restroom. When she comes back, she sees that her husband has left her an odd text message. When she takes a closer look, she realizes that her male colleagues texted her husband a lewd message about how she wants to meet him at home for a night of wild sex because she is "hot in her pants." (This is not the exact language used.) The guys at your table snicker as she reads her husband's response. You watched your male colleagues take her phone and text her husband, and you did nothing.

Take action if you see inappropriate behavior, and *don't be a bystander*. As a male colleague, your words carry great weight. As a female colleague, this is an opportunity to redirect and modify behavior. In any case, you will show your leadership qualities. "Hey, guys, this is not appropriate! I know you think this is funny, but what would you think if someone did that to your wife? And all of you are going along with this? Erase the message, and put her phone down." Remind them of the company playground rule: "Care for your playground members!"

COMPANY PLAYGROUND RULE #3

If You Get That "Uh-Oh" Feeling, Tell a Grown-Up You Trust!

Another playground rule comes to mind: "If you get that 'uh-oh' feeling, tell a grown-up you trust!" Whether you're a man or a woman, you'll know if certain acts make you uncomfortable. The behavior will make you uneasy or make the victim anxious or scared. If you are a witness and don't know the parties involved, tell a superior or report the behavior to HR. If a female colleague confides in you that she's receiving inappropriate communications from a fellow or a senior colleague, let her know you're available to help her. In male-dominated work environments especially, male support, encouragement, and assistance is paramount to effecting real change. It will take other men to help modify bad behavior. If she has her male colleagues' support, she is more likely to be successful in pursuing her complaint and more likely to deal with the issue and seek help. If you have a good relationship with the offender, offer to talk to him, and encourage him to correct his behavior. You could also encourage her to talk to him and to take you along as a corroborating witness. If the harassment has been frequent and does not stop despite multiple efforts, advise her to report him to HR, and offer to go with her as a witness. If all else fails and the violator isn't getting the message or taking warnings seriously, the following playground rule applies: "Stop taking recess; time for discipline!"

**COMPANY PLAYGROUND RULE #4**

**Stop Taking Recess; Time for Discipline!**

Let's take an example in which women are perpetrators. Imagine you, as a man, are a regular visitor at a company, and the female receptionist can't help but tell you each time you visit that you're very good looking and she wants to date you. She tries to give you her number, but you kindly refuse. She becomes more persistent with each visit, and you finally tell her you're not interested, you're already in a relationship, and to please stop her advances. You even tell her you'll report her if she does not stop. She refuses and becomes more animated with her attention, to the point where you're embarrassed to even get off the elevator. She doesn't believe your claim that you'll turn her in for flirting if she does not stop immediately. In this case, the man was very uncomfortable with her advances, and he finally reported her to HR. It was time to stop taking recess; it was time for discipline. The receptionist was moved to a different floor and a different job at the company.

If you're a colleague who has spoken to the violator on behalf of the victim, or if you're a bystander and a witness to the inappropriate behavior, consider going to HR and filing a complaint. If you're the victim, consider reporting the harassment to a colleague who's superior to the abuser, reporting to the CEO or board of directors, or filing a complaint with HR. If you are the victim and don't receive a response, or if HR or the company doesn't take action even though you followed the policies and procedures of the company in filing such complaint, consider litigation.

Women have the right to occupy a place in the Sandbox without the fear of sexual harassment. Women have the right to participate in and contribute to the success of a company. The same goes for men who are harassed. If you witness sexual harassment as a bystander, it is time for you step up and help the victims in your lives. We need your help!

# 7

# Our Call to Men: We Need Your Help to Effect Change

## The Importance of Male Support

JR and I have talked to many of our male family members, colleagues, and friends about their thoughts on sexual harassment and their reactions to many of the recent news stories. As you would guess, most seemed appalled and especially troubled by the more egregious behaviors, but there was also confusion about what crosses the line as inappropriate or risky and what to do if you are a bystander. We discovered there was unfamiliarity with the laws regarding sexual harassment and the policies and procedures that should be in place and enforced within their own companies. When we asked how many times they had attended a sexual harassment seminar at their company, many said "maybe once," and they did not find it particularly memorable.

To effect any real change concerning bad behavior, we need the support of the men in our lives and within our workforces. If we can help provide education and clarification regarding what is or is not appropriate, our men will be able to self-police and help modify and correct the bad behavior of others. Women do care about their men (of course!), and we do not want to see them get themselves into trouble any more than we want to be on the receiving end of something inappropriate. Many recent news stories involving incidents from decades ago—such as those regarding Roy Price (Amazon), Mike Halperin (NBC News), Paul Marciano (Guess cofounder), and Charlie Walk (music executive)—are likely to negatively impact an alleged violator's career, potentially for the rest of his life. It doesn't necessarily matter that you might be a changed person today.

Let's consider a few other examples . . .

In late 2017, radio newscaster Leeann Tweeden (Fox Sports Networks) accused US senator Al Franken (D-Minn.) of kissing and groping her without her consent in two separate incidents during a 2006 USO tour of the Middle East, prior to his becoming a senator shortly thereafter. According to Tweeden, during the rehearsal of a comedy skit written to involve a kiss, Franken forced a kiss with tongue, despite her objections and attempts to push him away. The groping was captured in a picture taken on the flight back from Afghanistan while Tweeden was asleep in her flak jacket and helmet—standard when traveling in military cargo planes. In the photo, Franken is grinning at the camera with his hands over her breasts. This picture is now widely circulated. Franken immediately apologized, claiming that the picture was made "as a joke" and that he remembered the rehearsal differently from the accounts Tweeden gave. In a personal letter to Tweeden, he said, "What is important is the impact it had on you, and you felt violated by my actions, and for that, I apologize."[1] Shortly after this news broke, Franken faced possible Senate Ethics Committee hearings.[2] He was later accused by several other women of similar behavior.[3]

The story has evolved into a great opportunity for discussion.

## Engaging Men in Discussion

A few years ago, I retired after thirty-plus years of practicing law. Since then, I've regularly joined my husband's Friday lunch group, which is composed of men who work primarily in the commercial real-estate / finance industry. At one of the lunches, Senator Franken was naturally a hot topic, and all men present at the lunch believed Franken's behavior toward Tweeden was inappropriate. Franken's use of tongue without warning or consent was troubling and, all echoed, an assault on her person. But what about the picture? Again, all of the men agreed that even if Franken thought the picture was meant in jest, Tweeden had not consented; what he did was disrespectful and demeaning, whether he touched her or not. I was glad these men recognized improper behavior and impressed with their willingness to share their opinions and concerns with me. Four of the five in the group have daughters in college and in the workforce. Sexual harassment has now become a regular topic at these lunches.

So it turned out I did not have to influence these men's opinions, but I questioned whether men generally agreed with this view. How could I test the waters to ask these men, who seemed more likely to know? At that particular lunch, I told them about an episode I had seen that morning of *Across America with Carol Costello* on the cable station HLN.[4] One of Castello's guests, conservative commentator John Ziegler, strenuously stated that Franken had only meant it as a joke and that America "had lost its mind." He went on to say that even his wife believed many of the #MeToo allegations were ridiculous. Costello, another male guest on her show, and I were surprised by his comment. Ziegler did not think Franken had crossed a line? The men at our Friday lunch were equally concerned by Ziegler's position. Why is it so difficult to understand that no means NO and "stop" means "STOP"? It does not matter that Franken meant the pictures as a joke. His behavior was not appropriate and was undertaken without her consent. Franken should have thought about how Tweeden might have perceived his behavior had she been awake. If given the opportunity, she would likely not have consented to taking the picture.

Ziegler refused to concede, even when asked if he would think differently had his wife or one of his two daughters been the targets of a similar prank. As fathers, brothers, sons, and colleagues of girls and women, the men in my lunch group all agreed: it's time to actively participate in effecting change and communicating to other men (both openly and behind closed doors) that sexual harassment must stop and will no longer be allowed or ignored. No means NO! Whoever took the Franken picture or any bystander present should have said something to the effect of, "Let's not take this picture. It's not appropriate, and she won't appreciate this as funny!" From what we have been told, however, no one did.

After further discussion at our lunch, the men at the table all committed to the following goal: regardless of whether the action is intended as harmless or funny, let's be more sensitive to how this type of behavior might affect the woman on the receiving end and how she might feel as its unfortunate recipient. No more excuses that this is just "locker-room talk" or that "boys will be boys." We should hold our men to a higher standard, and they should be held accountable for sexual harassment. It is time to "man up" to this movement (pun intended), lead by example, and help influence and educate men who engage in bad behavior that's disrespectful toward women or men. Let's unlearn bad behavior together and treat the opposite gender with civility and respect! We understand that, as a bystander, calling someone out in front of a group can be uncomfortable, especially if the violator is a superior. Embarrassing the violator in public might create an enemy, and if the person is your boss, you might risk your career. If the recipient of the behavior is part of a group, consider changing the subject, creating a distraction, or pulling the violator aside and talking to that person privately. If you are an equal or the superior, a gentle reprimand will be heard and will be a positive way to exhibit your leadership skills.

Don't miss an opportunity to discuss when behavior constitutes sexual harassment. You might have a positive influence. At a recent couples' dinner, one of the men made an improper comment about a nice-looking woman walking by the table. He did not seem concerned that his comment was loud enough for the wives at the table to hear him. We all raised eyebrows, and he became irritated. "Why can't I comment on a 'great ass' walking by if she can't hear me?" He didn't understand "all of the fuss." A lengthy discussion ensued, and he soon realized that the woman might not have appreciated his comment had she heard him.

JR recounts a similar story at a recent work meeting. During a break, the topic of the #MeToo movement came up, and an older male colleague blurted out, "Sexual harassment is important to women; to men, it is just like scratching an itch!" Similar to my friend at the couples' dinner, he didn't understand all the fuss, either.

JR retorted, "Did you hear what you just said? You have daughters who care about their careers. Surely you would not want them to suffer sexual harassment?" JR's colleague regrouped and decided JR was correct. He would not want his daughters to suffer sexual harassment. You have likely witnessed similar situations. These stories illustrate that there is much work to be done to educate and modify attitudes regarding sexual harassment and what type of behavior is not appropriate. We need men who care about this topic to actively participate in calling out bad behavior and educating other men on what is not appropriate.

## Common Motivations for Sexual Harassment

Some men mistakenly believe sexual harassment is, at some level, flattering to women—a form of acceptable flirting or courtship. If this were true, however, this type of "courtship" would be observably unsuccessful. As Langelan points out, "women react with disgust, not desire, with fear, not fascination. Any rational male, acting on a genuine desire to interest a possible sexual partner, would quickly realize that his best bet is to abandon this disastrous approach."[5]

It is well established that sexual harassment is not a form of acceptable flirting or courtship; rather, it is an expression of power intended to control the recipient's behavior. Like rape, sexual harassment is designed to coerce women, not attract them. As we have discussed earlier in this book, a person who commits sexual harassment has one or more motivations in mind. They may be an Ego Joe, motivated to boost his or her own ego—for example, a man in a group of men who vulgarly comments on women's bodies as they walk past. They may be Tyrant Ivan, seeking to force a woman to provide sexual services in exchange for her promotion or other work favors: "If you sleep with me, I will give you that promotion or let you work a high-profile project—quid pro quo." Or they may be Insecure Trip, who feels threatened by the potential competition—for example, he may cut off a female colleagues' attempts to contribute during a meeting by interrupting her or ignoring her comments. The violator might also try to intimidate and shake a woman's confidence to protect his turf or position at work by saying, "We have heard enough from the men. Let's let the girl with the tits have a word!" Regardless of the motivation for sexual harassment, male dominance and male bonding over women is psychologically fulfilling and is a behavior learned at an early age at home, at school, and in the community.[6] Despite current laws that makes this behavior illegal, it is still largely tolerated and often excused using a familiar expression: "boys will be boys."

Until violators realize that the potential risks associated with sexual harassment outweigh the ill-perceived benefits, it will be up to all of us—the men and women in the Sandbox—to continue effecting change to stop this behavior.

# Treat Others How You Want to Be Treated: The Golden Rule

Before you decide to make a comment about another person that is not appropriate, consider if you would be OK with that comment being directed to you, your mom, your sister, or your daughter. Ask yourself: How will that comment be perceived by the recipient? If you are a bystander and are listening to an inappropriate comment (about the body parts of a woman, for example), engage in the same exercise. Adopt the playground rule to "treat others how you want to be treated." If you are Ego Joe, don't make the comment in the first place; if you are a bystander, speak up, and say: "That comment isn't appropriate. You wouldn't want that being said about your daughter, would you?" If you are a fellow male colleague or a friend, Ego Joe will listen, and you will be on your way to helping in the fight to correct the problem.

Take advantage of the stories regarding sexual harassment that are pouring in from many industries. We have highlighted a few for you in this book for this purpose. You have an opportunity to open up and engage men and women in meaningful conversations. Discussions spark awareness and inspire participants to teach others. Both JR and I have been actively engaging in these conversations with men and women for decades, including with men who hold senior positions in their companies.

In one case, a senior executive of a particularly male-dominated company told us, "We don't have a sexual harassment problem. I don't see it in our daily interactions with our female colleagues." But after JR and I walked him through a few examples, drilling down on what types of interactions were common at similar companies, he realized that sexual harassment might be occurring. After further thought, the executive recalled and recounted to us a sales meeting he had had recently with a male customer and a young female colleague. His colleague was the expert on the product they were marketing to the customer, but she had difficulty keeping him focused, as he kept interrupting her with sexual innuendos and propositions that she go home with him after the meeting. On reflection, our executive friend admitted there was possibly something he could have done, but in the moment, he was not sure what to do, so he did not intervene on behalf of this young woman. We discussed a number of scenarios with ideas on how he might have handled the situation, and when we parted ways, we knew this executive would be better prepared going forward. The next time we visited, he had many more instances to share and recounted how he'd been able to handle them successfully.

If you can find time to have these important discussions, include the young men and women in your lives, and use examples from recent news. Our young men enter high school and college with insufficient guidance about handling peer pressure concerning sexual harassment, sexual assault, hazing, and bullying. The same is true for young women, who encounter sexual banter and innuendo, sexual predators, and bullies. There are plenty of news stories involving schools, universities, and the impact of such behavior on our children and young adults. If they survive their experiences in high school and college—and, sadly, I do mean "survive" literally in some circumstances—are our children fully prepared to enter the workforce? Will they be better informed and better protected than JR and I were when our generation entered the workforce thirty years ago? We hope that if we can have these discussions with our children early in their lives and teach them the playground rules and their applications through examples in the adult world, they will be much better prepared to handle sexual harassment, sexual assault, hazing, and bullying. As adults (and parents), we must be actively engaged in this conversation. Federal and state laws have not come far enough to eradicate such behavior in or outside of the workforce.

## An Important Historical Review

To promote a better understanding of how far women have come with women's rights and laws regarding sexual harassment in the workplace, the following section is a brief history.

For decades, women have suffered from sexually predatory behavior in the workforce, mostly in silence, and their complaints have been dismissed as trivial or harmless. Even the passage of Title VII of the Civil Rights Act of 1964,[7] which in large part prohibits sex discrimination and harassment in the workplace, did not eradicate bad behavior. If you did not like the behavior, you were encouraged to leave and find another job. It was better to suffer in silence than to jeopardize your job. Not until the mid-to-late 1970s, as the number of women in the workforce dramatically increased and women started sharing their experiences, did the campaign against sexual harassment gain fruitful support.[8]

In 1975, the phrase "sexual harassment" was termed by a group of women at Cornell University.[9] When a former employee of the university, Carmita Wood, filed a claim for unemployment benefits after resigning from her job due to unwanted touching from her supervisor, the university denied her request, reasoning that she had quit for "personal reasons." Activists at Cornell helped Wood form a group called "Working Women United," and after hosting an event where women could speak freely, women of varying professions—including secretaries, filmmakers, factory workers, and waitresses—shared their experiences, revealing that inappropriate, sexually harassing behavior such as pressure to trade sexual favors for job retention and promotions extended well beyond the university setting.[10] This event in May of 1975 was the first rally of its kind and received national attention. That August, the *New York Times* highlighted the issue to its broad circulation of readers by using the phrase "sexual harassment" in its headline.[11]

In 1976, *Redbook* sent a two-page questionnaire titled "How Do You Handle . . . Sex on the Job?" for their readers to fill out and mail back. Surveys were common for *Redbook*; this one, however, started an important conversation and provided the first nationwide statistics on sexual harassment at work, showing that nearly 90 percent of respondents had experienced one or more forms of unwanted attention on the job and that 92 percent of women said sexual harassment at work was a problem.[12] A few years later, in an article published May 1, 1981, *Time* magazine reported that according to the Washington-based research group the Center for Women Policy Studies, as many as eighteen million American females were harassed sexually while at work in 1979 and 1980.[13] In the popular 1980 comedy *9 to 5*, starring Dolly Parton, Lily Tomlin, and Jane Fonda, Hollywood addressed the issue by showing three working women exacting revenge on their sexist boss. As expected, with greater discussion of the issue came pushback. This same *Time* article also reported that "antifeminist crusader" Phyllis Schlafly believed that most of the eighteen million women claiming sexual harassment were "asking for it."[14] At a later Senate committee hearing to review federal guidelines on sexual harassment, Schlafly testified that "virtuous women are seldom accosted."[15] It took dedicated feminist attorneys to move the issue forward, including professor Catherine MacKinnon, who pioneered legal theories of sexual harassment for successful use in state and federal court litigation ("hostile working environment" and "quid pro quo," such as sex for promotion), as well as Eleanor Holmes Norton, director of the EEOC, who was principally influential in revamping the law regarding workplace equality by recognizing that sexual harassment violated women's rights.

By 1977, several important court cases ruled that a woman could sue her employer for sexual harassment under Title VII of the Civil Rights Act of 1964[16] and under the Equal Employment Opportunity Commission.[17] In 1986, the US Supreme Court recognized harassment as a form of illegal sex discrimination.[18] A number of high-profile cases followed, including Anita Hill's testimony against US Supreme Court nominee Clarence Thomas in 1991. Hill testified before a Judiciary Committee composed entirely of men, claiming Thomas had engaged in inappropriate sexual behavior when she worked for him at the Education Department and again later when he was chairman of the EEOC (Equal Employment Opportunity Commission). Her testimony and her treatment during the hearings sparked renewed outrage and discussion on the subject of sexual harassment. From 1991 to 1996, the number of sexual harassment complaints filed with the Equal Employment Opportunity Commission doubled[19] from 6,127 to 15,342, and the number of awards to victims under federal laws nearly quadrupled, increasing from $7.7 million to $27.8 million.[20] This public outcry helped place four women in Senate seats, including Carol Moseley Braun and Dianne Feinstein, who broke the all-male hold on the Senate Judiciary Committee. The year 1992 was named "The Year of the Woman" when a record twenty-four women were elected to the House and hundreds more ran for state legislatures, school boards, and county positions.[21]

In 1991, a sex scandal rocked the nation that almost cost President Clinton his presidency. Clinton was accused by Paula Jones of sexual harassment when he was governor of Arkansas. She claimed Clinton had exposed himself and asked her for oral sex in a hotel room at a conference they were attending. After four and a half years of legal warfare, Jones settled her charge for a startling $850,000, without any acknowledgment of wrongdoing and without apology from Clinton. Jones's allegations opened the door to investigating the president's sex life when she subpoenaed Monica Lewinsky over Lewinsky's relationship and alleged affair with President Clinton while she was his twenty-one-year-old intern. When the story broke, the allegations were shocking to the nation. Clinton publicly denied the allegations with his famous words, "I did not have sexual relations with that woman, Ms. Lewinsky."[22] The Monica Lewinsky scandal almost cost Clinton his presidency. Clinton was impeached by the House of Representatives on two counts—not for his alleged sexual encounters with Lewinsky, but rather for lying under oath to a federal grand jury and for obstructing justice. He later admitted to having an "inappropriate relationship with Monica Lewinsky" and was acquitted by the Senate in his impeachment trial by a small majority.[23]

Then came what was considered the worst case of sexual harassment in US Naval history—the Tailhook scandal, involving sexual allegations against the armed forces.[24] Drunken naval and marine corps officers of the Tailhook Association (a private group of retired and active-duty naval aviators) attending an annual conference at Vegas's Hilton Hotel assaulted eighty women, including then navy lieutenant Paula Coughlin. According to reports, the navy paid more than $190,000 to fly fifteen hundred officers on military aircraft to Las Vegas.[25] The resulting scandal forced the resignation of the secretary of the navy, the temporary freeze by Congress of forty-five hundred navy promotions, and the implementation of reforms that stressed a zero-tolerance policy. Sean O'Keefe, the new navy secretary, instituted gender sensitivity classes, closed officer drinking clubs, and started a commission to study whether women should serve on combat ships and planes.[26] Despite a blistering report from the Pentagon and 140 officers facing possible punishment, no one was criminally prosecuted.

Coughlin later claimed her employer failed to investigate her allegations and then retaliated against her for being a whistleblower. The case highlighted how hostile the military was to women and what women had been experiencing for years—the military's silent epidemic. For example, in 2012, the Pentagon reported 3,374 sexual assault cases but estimated that about 26,000 had actually taken place. Only 9 percent of assault cases investigated in 2012 ended in convictions.[27] These statistics do not address men who are sexually assaulted in the military. The Tailhook scandal involved seven men who were assaulted. Coughlin ended up filing a lawsuit against the Vegas Hilton for failing to provide adequate security, with which a jury ultimately agreed, awarding Coughlin $1.7 million in compensatory and $5 million in punitive damages.[28] Later that year, Congress passed the 1991 amendment to the Civil Rights Act, providing greater remedies for victims, including the right to trial by a jury of their peers under Title VII of the Civil Rights Act of 1964[29] and the right to compensatory and punitive damages as a result of the harassment. Notwithstanding the statistics regarding sexual assault in the military, women who serve have Coughlin to thank for two very positive changes resulting from the Tailhook scandal. Two years later, the navy and air force opened most combat jobs to women, and in 2013, women were permitted to serve in ground combat.[30]

Continuing with historical developments in the law, in 1994, victims were permitted to introduce a violator's history of past sexually inappropriate and harassing behavior as evidence, while a violator's ability to enter evidence about the victim's consensual sexual history as a defense (essentially pleading guilty but arguing that "she was asking for it" because she was otherwise sexually active) was limited. The law passed was called the Violence Against Women Act.[31] Then, in 1998, the Supreme Court confirmed "quid pro quo" sexual harassment (demanding sexual favors in exchange for advancement or other work benefits) in two landmark cases—*Burlington Industries, Inc. v. Ellerth* and *Faragher v. City of Boca Raton*—holding that employers were liable for sexual harassment even if threats and favors weren't followed through with. These cases also established certain defenses to employer liability if the employer could prove that they took prompt action to prevent the harassment and to respond to harassment claims.[32]

With the new changes in the law, more and more companies began to implement sexual harassment policies, procedures, and training to foster compliance. However, despite the vast improvements in the law and actions taken by companies to implement zero-tolerance policies, sexual harassment continued to be alive and well.

Another important case involved the car manufacturer Mitsubishi. In 1998, Mitsubishi agreed to pay $34 million (and several more million under individual suits) to hundreds of female workers at the Norma, Illinois, plant for allowing a hostile working environment for women that began in 1990 and included routine verbal abuse, obscene jokes and graffiti, fondling, and other offensive behavior. Many women were forced to quit, and others were denied promotions when they refused to grant sexual favors. The settlement was one of the largest on record in a corporate case at the time.[33]

In 2001, two women filed an action against the University of Colorado, claiming they had been sexually assaulted at an off-campus party thrown for football players and recruits and charging the university's football program with fostering a culture of sexual assault. The lawsuit was filed under Title IX of the Education Amendments of 1972,[34] which protects women from gender harassment and discrimination in education programs, and claimed the football program was inappropriately trying to attract the best male high school prospects with "sex-and-alcohol parties" without regard to the safety of female students.[35]

Six years after the original complaint was filed, the University of Colorado announced it would pay $2.85 million to settle the lawsuits after the university was ordered by a federal appeals court to stand trial on charges that the university's officials had failed to take appropriate action to prevent the alleged assault. The lawsuits had a devastating impact on the university, resulting in the firing of the system's then president, chancellor, athletic director, and football coach. The university committed to making changes and hiring new leadership, overhauled its athletic program to enact strict recruitment policies, and implemented more stringent sexual harassment policies and procedures for its students.[36]

The preceding cases are significant in the sense that they should have set a tone—in our highest positions of government, our federal agencies, the military, corporate America, and our colleges and universities—of what not to do going forward. They were essential examples to spark discussion, encourage behavior modification, and require real changes within our laws and from the top down, such as policies prohibiting sexual harassment, strict accountability and penalties for violation, regular training regarding appropriate behavior, and support for victims.

However, as we already know, sexual harassment and assault have continued in the working environments of our government, corporate America, in our colleges and universities, in Hollywood, and in most other major industries, remaining front and center in our news almost every single day.

## Pillar Suggestions on How Men Can Help

### 1.   Don't Be a Bystander. Take Action to Correct Bad Behavior.

If you are witness to inappropriate behavior toward a woman, say something at that very moment. "Hey, guys, that is disrespectful and not appropriate. You are making her uncomfortable!" Or, if men in your presence say derogatory or demeaning things about a woman walking by: "If she heard you, that would make her very uncomfortable." You might add, "Heck, you are making me uncomfortable. Let's stop that kind of talk right now!" If you witness a male colleague or superior acting inappropriately with a female subordinate (for example, putting his arm around her shoulder or waist while she is clearly uncomfortable), please intervene. Tell your colleague, "Hey, Tyrant Ivan, I don't think she appreciates you touching her. Please let her go, and keep your hands to yourself! You are violating company policy, and we don't want anyone getting into trouble." If you are concerned about putting the violator on the defensive, find a way to distract him and interrupt his behavior. Say, "Hey, Sally, let's go make that call we were planning," or "Sally, I found that email I wanted to show you," or "Sally, I have the document you wanted to see on my computer." Then pull her away from Tyrant Ivan. Say anything that might get her out of the situation.

If you know the violator on a more personal level, or if you are a superior, interrupt the violator, pull him aside, and let him know that his behavior is not appropriate. Tell him that his actions violate company policy and that he is risking getting in trouble with HR. If a male colleague tells a dirty joke, say, "Seriously? Ego Joe, that is vile. People don't want to hear that. Go wash your mouth with soap!" Shut that person down immediately; doing so with humor works very well. In every case, remind them of these very important playground rules we first learned as children: "Respect the playground and its players! Treat others how you want to be treated! Inappropriate treatment of players is strictly prohibitied!" If you take corrective action immediately, you're more likely to make an impact and quash any such future behavior. Men will listen to other men and take notice. Set an example, and change the culture to one of mutual respect. If you take action to correct others, you'll be able to self-police your actions and comments as well. As Martin Luther King Jr. once said, "In the end, what will hurt the most is not the words of our enemies, but the silence of our friends!"

## 2. Be a Fierce Ally of Women

If the abuser does not seem interested in self-correction and continues the bad behavior despite multiple warnings from the victim, or if you discover that a colleague is being sexually harassed by another colleague and the victim is not comfortable confronting her abuser (whether a superior or not), talk to the harassed colleague. Offer to discuss her options regarding how to handle the situation, and let her know that if she decides to pursue a formal complaint, you're her ally and will speak out for her as a witness. If she is not interested in filing a complaint, offer to talk to the abuser or to his superior to see if the bad behavior can be resolved without filing a complaint. She should decide her preference. If you talk to the abuser but he continues his bad behavior, then move to Plan

B, and talk to HR. The violator should be held accountable for his behavior.

### 3. Don't Be Afraid to Talk about Sexual Harassment with Your Colleagues, Friends, or Family Members

The #MeToo movement and the watershed of stories that have surfaced as a result are causing conversation and positive changes with respect to raising awareness and implementing corrective action within many of our industries. Take advantage of this movement for a better understanding so you can help eradicate bad behavior. Ask your female colleagues and friends about their experiences and what they believe constitutes behavior that crosses the line. Gain a better understanding about why women have waited for years—often decades—to talk about their experiences. Understand, however, that these experiences are often very painful, and unless you know that person well, she may not be willing or comfortable sharing details. Ask these women what you can learn from their experiences. Maybe you can help by suggesting how they can reject such behavior without getting an angry or career-ending reaction. After all, men do know men best, and keep in mind that simply punching the abuser in the face may not be a good option for a woman.

### 4. Ask Women for Guidance on How You Can Help

In your discussions with women, ask them how you can help with what might be happening at work with colleagues. Are there current abusers in the office? In the women's opinion, does the office foster an environment of sexual harassment? Is HR doing its job with respect to claims that have been filed and the enforcement of policies and procedures? Are abusers being appropriately punished or fired? Are complainants experiencing retaliation of any kind? Is there adequate sexual harassment training, and is this training being taken seriously?

## 5. Take a Look at Your Own Training in Sexual Harassment

We understand that there is confusion about what constitutes inno-cent flirting and what crosses the line into sexual harassment. We also know that, in many cases, violators think they are being funny and are not intending to demean, disrespect, or hurt the target. Yet men manage to do it every single day, and, sadly, women do it as well. Demand that your employer hire an experienced professional to review your company's internal policies and procedures, to assess whether the HR employees handling these types of claims are prop-erly trained, and to hold regular quarterly seminars for the staff and executives. Make sure this training pays special attention to men and women in leadership positions and addresses the issues of bystanders and unconscious bias. Proper education and awareness regarding conduct that crosses the line will make it much easier to identify and deal with violators. More importantly, your abused colleague or staff member will receive greater support and hopefully will not have to worry about retaliation or losing her job. She will feel more comfortable staying with the company knowing that the company is in her corner.

As a male in the work environment, you have an opportunity to be a leader and an example to other men. Men will listen to men. Show your strength, courage, moral integrity, and good character as a gentleman. You owe this to the women in your lives—and to your sons! Teach them that women are not objects or toys; they are human beings. Keep in mind that men also experience discriminatory behavior, including sexual harassment. Similar action should be taken to protect the men in your environment.

## Examples of Behavior That Is Not Acceptable: What Constitutes Crossing the Line?

### 1. If You Wouldn't Do It to a Man

Apparently, confusion reigns among some men about what's improper behavior and when they're crossing the line. But is it that difficult? We're not worried about clumsy compliments such as, "I like your dress—um—showing skin—um." Just say, "I like your dress," although it's generally best to refrain from commenting on women's clothing at work, at a company function, or in the presence of colleagues. Be professional. In this scenario, the woman wore a dress that showed skin at the top of her shoulders. She wasn't offended and knew what her male coworker meant, but she later commented to us women that she could have avoided the situation by not showing any skin at all—she was at a company dinner with clients and was likely violating the company's dress code. She felt she had a responsibility regarding what she wore at work, at company functions, and around her male colleagues. We will talk about this subject later in this book.

Men must understand that women are not worried about clumsy comments. What women worry about are predatory comments or behavior—comments that are disrespectful, intimidating, degrading, or insulting. Egregious behavior with ulterior motives. We recently read, "It's almost as if men can't do anything right. You [men] shouldn't be afraid of saying or doing something because it could be misinterpreted as the wrong thing. You should be afraid of saying or doing a wrong thing and having it be interpreted in exactly the way you meant it."[37]

We agree.

Not too long ago, a female cadet at a military academy returned to her classroom desk to find what appeared to be a used condom tucked in her book binder. She heard snickering and some laughter as she absorbed her discovery. Yes, there were a bunch of Ego Joes in the room. As calmly as she could, she looked up from her binder and said, "Hilarious, guys!" Her reaction was solid. She wasn't going to give the men the satisfaction that their behavior troubled her. Undoubtedly, this was not her first experience, and as we all know, it won't be her last. So, even though her response might have communicated that she wasn't bothered, how does she shut down the violator's behavior permanently? She could take the condom, hold it up for all to see, and say with a smile, "Someone in this group has an overinflated view of his assets!" The guys would likely laugh and think she's a good sport, but they may not be deterred from continuing to test her tolerance.

How do you, as a female professional, communicate "a line of tolerance" that shouldn't be crossed? You don't want your colleagues to get the sense you're weak and can't handle male coworkers, so running out of the room and telling HR might not be your best option. You may not want to angrily admonish them, either, since you're likely to alienate them and risk your future career (and, if you care, your ability to be a member of the boys' club). The following playground rules come to mind:

Consider the following: take the condom, stand it up for everyone to see, and gently say with a smile, "I wonder if our sergeant would be impressed with our class activities?" Or how about, "You're furthering the #MeToo movement. Our sergeant would not be impressed." Or, "I doubt the academy would think this is being respectful of your female colleagues. Don't we have sexual harassment policies?" Or, "Really, guys? What if I was your sister? Your daughter? Or your mother? Would you want them to be disrespected? Not cool! This is not polite or good manners!" Remind them of the following playground rule: "Respect the playground and its players!" Then, for all to see, take the condom, wrap it in a piece of paper (or a plastic bag, if you have one), and put it in your bag—to indicate you might be holding on to it. Any of these responses would be a gentle admonishment and communicate that you now have evidence of sexual harassment without making an open threat to turn them into HR or to the sergeant. If you can, take a few notes regarding the date and witnesses in case you need this information at a later date.

To our fellow men, a recent column said it perfectly: "If you wouldn't do it to a man, don't do it."[38] If you're a man, would you be OK with another man pressing his package against the front of your pants or kissing you on the mouth and putting his tongue down your throat? What about a man putting his hand down your pants? Or—well, you get the picture. Simply said, if you wouldn't do it to a man, then don't do it to a woman. Does that help? (Though we do know a few men who have been accused of similar behavior toward other men—high-powered talent agent Adam Venit, for example, and actor Kevin Spacey.)

## 2. Revisiting the Playground Rules: What Is Bad Behavior?

Let's get back to your childhood playground. Picture yourself at age seven with your friends, both boys and girls. Did you have any playground rules? Maybe you had them in lower school? We find that many of them are applicable to adults in the workplace and may help illustrate what's inappropriate behavior that should be prohibited in your company's sexual harassment policies.

As you study each rule, review the examples of behavior we believe violates the rule by constituting sexual harassment.

**PLAYGROUND**
**RULE #1**

Respect the
Playground and
Its Players

• Looking at or commenting on a woman's body in a way that makes her uncomfortable. There's a difference between saying, "Nice dress," and saying, "That dress shows off your curves." If your target is uncomfortable or resistant, stop.

• Unwanted repeated compliments.

• Violating a woman's space without her explicit permission. Don't stand too close, and don't touch. Keep your hands to yourself.

• Talking about your own sexual experiences.

• Telling a woman what she needs to do to get laid or "lucky," or telling her she needs to relax and get laid or "lucky."

• Telling a woman what guys like on a date.

• Referring to a woman's breasts or other physical traits. Don't do this—*ever*.

• Telling a woman she "needs to smile more." Her purpose is not to be pretty or to smile more.

• If a woman is not interested in your advances (she asks you to stop, says no, or is visibly uncomfortable or shaken by your advances), *stop* and back off *immediately*.

PLAYGROUND
**RULE #2**

Treat Others
How You Want
to Be Treated

- Asking the female colleague in the room to undertake tasks demeaning to her position (fetching coffee, making copies, taking notes).
- Calling the female colleague "girl," "babe," or "honey." Anything other than her real name, requested name, or her company title is not appropriate.
- Making degrading comments about a female colleague in front of others.
- Treating a female colleague with disrespect.
- Not giving a woman credit when deserved.
- Ignoring or dismissing a female colleague and/or her contributions.

- Cutting off, interrupting, or purposefully ignoring female colleagues in meetings.
- Dismissing the skill sets, experience, and education of your female colleagues.
- Purposefully excluding a female colleague while planning meetings in her presence.
- Telling others in a women's presence that women are not as intelligent or hardworking as men or that they are too emotional.
- Making unreasonable demands on female subordinates.
- Badgering or being rude to your female subordinates.

PLAYGROUND
**RULE #3**

No Bullying or
Intimidation
Allowed

**PLAYGROUND RULE #4**

Use Nice Words, Be Polite, and Have Good Manners

- Off-color jokes. Know your audience.
- Sexually explicit language or sexual innuendos, whether you whisper them or send them in an email, tweet, message, or text.
- Sexist and demeaning comments about women, whether they can hear you or not.
- Whistling at a woman—it objectifies her body.
- Flashing your private parts without the subject's consent.
- Looking a woman up and down intensely, with or without groaning.

---

- While on a trip out of town, demanding that your female colleague or subordinate attend meetings in your hotel room.
- Exposing her to pornographic materials (or leaving them open and in plain sight on your desk or your computer).
- Asking about or commenting on a woman's sex life, in a text or otherwise.
- Sending a female colleague inappropriate emails, texts, or social media messages or posts.
- Allowing clients to flirt or engage in inappropriate behavior with your female colleagues or subordinates.
- Rating coworkers on a "hot scale" of one to ten.

**PLAYGROUND RULE #5**

Respect the Boundaries of the Players

**PLAYGROUND**
**RULE #6**

**Work Together to Solve Problems, Using Your Words, Not Your Hands**

• Asking your female colleague to give you a neck rub or massage to help you relax while you are working.

• Massaging your secretary's shoulders or neck.

• Grabbing a part of your female colleague's body during a meeting to see how she will react.

• Inviting a female colleague to your place after hours to complete a project, or forcing her to come, "since it will be more comfortable for all involved."

---

• Touching of any kind. No forced hugs.

• Trying to have a woman meet you alone, outside of work, for purposes you wouldn't share with your wife, boss, or mother.

• If you're traveling, asking a woman to meet you alone in your hotel room for sexual purposes.

• Asking a female colleague to handle inappropriate menial tasks.

• Telling a woman what to wear to a meeting or using her as a prop at a client event.

**PLAYGROUND**
**RULE #7**

**Inappropriate Treatment of Players Is Strictly Prohibited**

**PLAYGROUND RULE #8**

**We Share Playground Resources and Take Turns**

- Interrupting or cutting off a female colleague when she is speaking.
- Ignoring a female colleague's efforts to contribute to a meeting or to do anything related to work.
- Refusing to give projects to a female subordinate because she's a woman.
- Excluding female colleagues from strategy sessions and other meetings with team members or clients.

---

- Ignoring new members of the team, especially if they're women.
- Degrading new members of the group without giving them the opportunity to prove themselves.

**PLAYGROUND RULE #9**

**New Players Are Welcome**

---

**PLAYGROUND RULE #10**

**Do Not Jump off the Seesaw without Warning Your Playmate**

- Leaving an unsuspecting colleague or staffer with another male colleague who, based on comments he has made, you think is interested in a "score" or has another less honorable intention.
- Forcing/instigating kisses or hugs between a colleague and your customer or client because you think that is what your customer or client wants.

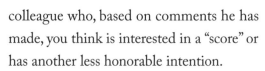

### 3. Understand Her Body Language

Specific encounters can be confusing. Say you invite a female colleague into your office after hours or to your hotel room on a company trip to discuss business. If she enters and you close the door without objection from her, don't assume this means she's interested in a sexual relationship. Remember that she is a work colleague, and if you're her boss or senior to her, she may be worried about possibly affecting her career by objecting. In these instances, you're in a position of power over her career. Don't be Tyrant Ivan. Conversely, if you are the female (or male target) in this situation and you think your colleague may have sexual intentions, clarify gently that you are not interested in any sexual relationship. Communicate if any activity is making you uncomfortable, and do not hesitate to add that, because you are a subordinate or a work colleague, such behavior is not appropriate and likely violates company policies regarding sexual harassment.

The foregoing example is different from going on a date with someone who is not a colleague. If you're in a comparable situation with a person you do not work with, we hope your date will be clear about any intentions you might have. However, even in this situation, you may get confusing responses, or that person may be intimidated, reserved, or insecure about relationships. A recent date involving actor Aziz Ansari (of the Netflix series *Master of None*) and reported in explicit detail by an anonymous female called "Grace" was criticized as not being a "valid" #MeToo story. Public outcry deemed her experience a "bad date"—one that did not live up to her expectations. She was criticized for sending Ansari mixed messages regarding his sexual advances. In this case, she wasn't looking for a job, and he wasn't in a position of power over her career. Yes, he is a celebrity, and she may have been intimidated or looking for a meaningful or long-term relationship. According to her critics, exposing him in public not only humiliated him but also unfairly jeopardized his career. As Grace describes, she texted him regarding her uncomfortable experience the next day in response to a text from him that said, in part, "It was fun meeting you." He immediately expressed his sorrow for her experience and apologized for misreading her.[39]

Whether you agree with Grace or not, she could have been more forceful and said, "No, we are not having sex tonight! Stop touching me. This is our first date, and I am just getting to know you. Let's take this slow." Or, when she'd had enough, she could have said, "I am going home. This is not what I was expecting." She could have shut him down and left, plain and simple. Conversely, he should have been more attuned to her reluctance (or indecisiveness) and stopped his advances. She was obviously not sure how she wanted to respond to him. In her explicit and detailed account, one thing was obvious: she was not an enthusiastic participant, and consent seems spotty. Yes, for some men, the male libido and the instinct to keep trying for sex tend to override rational thinking—but why have sex with someone who is not 100 percent on board? Why didn't Ansari pick up on her confusing reluctance, and why did he try to convince her anyway?

Men, it's simple. We believe the following applies to any date you have with a woman. If there's *any* sign she doesn't want sex (meaning the signals are not clear, verbally or physically, that she 100 percent wants sex) yet you keep pushing, you are verging on misconduct. In a work setting, the company will likely have a policy against sexual harassment, and personal relationships between colleagues may be strictly prohibited. If a woman's reaction to your comment or advance, whether verbal or physical, seems reluctant or negative, then trust her response. Does she appear uncomfortable? Is she looking away or averting her eyes? Is she pushing you away? Is her body language rejecting your advance? Is she verbalizing the word no? If the answer to any of these questions is yes, then abort immediately, and apologize for making her uncomfortable. That you thought you were being funny is no excuse. Nor is that you didn't intend to be offensive, that you thought she welcomed or had consented to your advance, or that her clothes appeared "inviting of your advance." Pay attention to her reaction. That is all you must do. Read her body language. Women do not mean yes when their behavior is showing reluctance, indecisiveness, or telling you no. *It is about the recipient and how your comment or advance personally impacts her.*

For example, if she is attracted to you, when you flirt with her (by, for example, brushing her arm while you are having drinks or staring at her longingly), she may not move your hand, back away, or find an excuse to leave your side. However, if she's not attracted to you, her reaction to your advance will advise accordingly. She might look away with disgust, move your hand away from her, or leave your side. *Take the time to appreciate her response to your advance.* Most importantly, if she is unable to consent (for example, she has her back to you and can't see you, she's walking by and can't hear you, she's sleeping, or she is passed out or intoxicated as a result of alcohol consumption), assume in every case that what you're doing is *not* appropriate and is *without* her consent. The British came out with a humorously instructive "cup of tea" video concerning this topic, which we highly recommend. Please take a look.[40] If you're still not sure what's appropriate, ask yourself how your mother, wife, daughter, or sister would react if you told them about your questionable behavior. Ask yourself how you would feel if this behavior were directed at one of them. Someone told me recently, "I would be proud if my daughter were paid attention to like that." Seriously? Are you sure? I would challenge any father to give this response more thought.

What makes this more difficult is that certain situations may seem innocent or intended as a kind gesture or compliment, but, in fact, they are not. Despite your intent, you may be making the recipient and/or the group of bystanders uncomfortable. Here is a recent example. You are at a gala, standing with a group of friends. A man comes up behind a woman in the group who is facing her husband, and he gently kisses her on the neck. You can tell the gesture makes her uncomfortable.

She immediately turns around, and it turns out that the man is someone she recognizes. They briefly hug. The man is later introduced as a pastor. Even if any member of the group could have mustered a comment regarding the kiss on the neck, they would likely have been surprised to learn his profession. He may have thought his kiss was innocent, but it was wholly inappropriate, all the more so considering his profession and position in his community.

Recently, one of our male friends recounted a situation in which he had lunch with several female colleagues. A regular of the group was on maternity leave. A comment he made about the negative impact of maternity leave on a female's future career made the women at the table uncomfortable. He picked up on the adverse reaction but chose not to ask what, specifically, about his comment made them uncomfortable. He wasn't sure what to say and told me that he's always cautious not to offend women. He has two daughters of his own. His colleagues at the table had missed an opportunity. If JR or I had been at the table, we would have gently asked if we could discuss his comment and then explained our concerns. We would have reminded him of the company's maternity policy and the importance of her returning to work without experiencing any losses or retribution. We would have reminded him that Title VII was amended in 1978 with the Pregnancy Discrimination Act to make it unlawful for employers to discriminate against pregnant women. The company might even have explicit guidelines in this regard.[41] It might be realistic that, upon his female colleague's return to work, she might have lost ground concerning her experience; however, per the company's policies, the company and her superiors are required to make every effort to catch her up.

If you are the woman at the table, don't be afraid to ask for a discussion to express your concerns and to educate your male colleague. If you are the man, be prepared to listen and accept the education. Having these types of talks every chance we get is imperative. How else will men understand the issues of gender imbalance? If you sense that the women at the table are uncomfortable asking for a discussion—which is to be expected if you are the male superior—ask them about their uncomfortable reaction. Apologize for your insensitive comment, and encourage them to explain their concerns. These women will certainly welcome your interest in correcting yourself, especially if you're genuine. You'll be viewed as a male leader who cares about the women in the workforce. As we have seen from the latest news, women are afraid to challenge a superior because it could impact their careers. More importantly, if you're in a leadership role, take the time to educate yourself on the laws of maternity leave and any policies that may be in place at your company, including any sexual harassment policies and procedures. If your company does not host regular educational seminars on these topics, ask that they be implemented immediately and regularly—at least twice a year and certainly for new employees.

In another example, when talk at the table turned to female career advancement, a senior male colleague said, "Women who want to succeed or become CEO have penis envy!"

JR, who was present, immediately called him out. "Ego Joe! Did you hear what you just said? What about your daughters? Wouldn't you want them to succeed and become CEO someday?" His daughters are both the sole breadwinners in their families.

He became defensive and said, "That is totally different!"

JR retorted, "Really? How so?"

He hadn't thought about how his comment might relate to his daughters, whether they were the sole breadwinners or not. "Of course my daughters deserve equal treatment," he responded.

How many times have we heard, "Women shouldn't be working! They should stay home and cook for the family!" The same question about the speaker's daughter applies. Any father who respects his daughter would want her to have equal opportunity to any man.

## 4. Understand the Statistics—They Don't Lie

At a recent dinner, one of the men with two college-aged daughters said, "Today, women represent more than 50 percent of the students in colleges and graduate schools. Women are also equally or more greatly represented in the job market and will be taking over the world before we know it!" The other men in the group agreed, and for them, the matter was settled. Women had finally achieved what they had always wanted—equality. The women at the dinner pulled out their phones and started researching statistics. Here they are: as of January 2018, approximately 66 percent of the workforce was male, and 54.6 percent was female (reporting differences account for the total not equaling 100 percent).[42] Nearly 50 percent of men think women are well represented in leadership in companies where only one in ten senior leaders is a woman.[43] Comparing the wages of women to those of white men dollar for dollar, white women are paid 81 cents on the dollar, Asian women are paid 88 cents on the dollar, African American women are paid 65 cents on the dollar, and Hispanic women are paid only 59 cents on the dollar.[44]

## 5. Women's Clothing and Sexual Harassment

Another question we heard recently from a man was troubling: "If women do not want to be sexually harassed, then why do they make themselves look so attractive and sexy?" Men, if you think about the question, you are saying that these women are asking to be violated. Believe it or not, women you might not think are beautiful or sexy are sexually harassed as well. According to psychologist Sandra Shullman, PhD, "Women's wardrobes have long been used as an excuse for sex crimes, however, when you look at the data on why people rape, that doesn't hold up . . . Victims were wearing a range of outfits from revealing to snowsuits . . . These are arguments to transfer the responsibility of control and power from the perpetrator to the victim."[45]

Notwithstanding this, there are findings that illustrate the persistent belief that women who wear revealing, provocative, or tight-fitting clothes are inviting sexual attention, making the female partially responsible for her assault and her attacker less culpable.[46] Jessica Wolfendale's paper explains how this belief is false and how there is no direct connection between a woman's choice to wear revealing clothing and a desire for sexual attention from men.[47] If, however, this belief remains widely held, should women bear a responsibility to not invite unwanted sexual attention from men and avoid the risk of potentially sending a "wrong" message? Is it imprudent for a woman not to exercise "self-protection," given the pervasive view that provocative clothing might risk sexual harassment? Maybe, at least until we have changed the view on this subject. However, how would you be able to understand, from one man to another, whether a man might interpret your clothing sexually? Not fair to women, is it? There are many reasons why a woman might dress in an attractive or sexy manner. She may want to look her best or feel more confident. She may be looking to follow current trends in fashion or exploring new styles. She may even want to turn on her partner or be looking to attract a potential date. Men do the very same, and yet no man would appreciate a guy pulling out his penis and masturbating in response.

Unfortunately, we have to advise women to be realistic. At work, whether you are a woman or a man, it is best to follow the company's dress code. Everywhere else? A woman should use good judgment. "Common sense dictates that a professional image doesn't include push-up bras with low cut or tight blouses, skirts so short that you have to continually tug at them when you sit down or bend over and dresses or pants that you have to pour yourself into."[48]

Regardless of the situation and how the woman may have dressed, nothing should mitigate or excuse sexual harassment behavior. The violator alone made the decision to sexually harass and should be held accountable for the consequences.

## 6. Why Are Women—Even Today—Rarely in Positions of Power?

The way JR handled her colleagues in the stories described above took courage and helped her draw a hard line of respect for her as a female broker. The respect she fostered and continued to encourage helped promote her career. Back then, there were very few women in commercial real-estate broker positions, let alone women working on larger industrial transactions. We firmly believe women are equally as intelligent and creative in resourcing and closing business transactions successfully, so why do they remain in the minority? It's simple. Some men continue to be hampered by traditional beliefs that women do not have the stamina, mental fortitude, intellect, or wit to contribute, negotiate, or close successful transactions. They believe women are not able to perform equal to or better than the men in their professions and should be staying home to cook, clean, and take care of the children. If they encounter a strong, talented, and competent woman who can hold her own, they are threatened by her as competition.[49] We believe this is true in almost every industry.

Certain men who feel threatened will protect their turf through intimidation and discrimination by engaging in disrespectful and demeaning behavior. This behavior might include ridiculing or openly ignoring women at meetings; assigning them tasks below their positions; demanding sexual favors; making aggressive sexual innuendo and commentary about women's dress, looks, and body language; and excluding women during interactive sessions, lunches, and events attended by male colleagues and clients (such as men's clubs after meetings and dinners). For example, in a recent case involving the popular athletic-wear company Nike, eleven senior executives and managers to date have been dismissed for partipating in, promoting, or condoning inappropriate behavior at Nike, including sexual language, forcible kissing, humiliating visits to strip clubs, exclusion from the inner circle of decision makers, and acts hindering career advancement of female employees. The behavior was brought to the attention of management after a group of women inside Nike's Beaverton, Oregon, headquarters delivered the results of a survey conducted among Nike's female employees that noted rampant sexual harassment and gender discrimination. Uproar followed, and a comprehensive internal investigation was launched. Apparently, prior complaints to HR had been largely ignored, dismissed, or resulted in retaliatory layoffs.[50]

This type of behavior has not changed and is alive and well today in every industry's workforce. Believe it or not, this type of behavior is also perpetrated by women—against other women and against men.[51] Our guess is that it will not take long for female perpetrators to be reported. A recent report allegedly involves one of Fox News's *The Five*, Kimberly Guilfoyle, who left the network after an internal investigation following misconduct that allegedly included emotional abuse of certain staff and showing photos of male genitalia. None of the sources claiming this alleged misconduct revealed themselves publicly, raising issues of veracity.[52] One of the reasons noted for why they remained anonymous was fear of retaliation or punishment. Regardless of the reason, when you (male or female) are the target of harassment, *how you react to this type of behavior* can impact the rest of your career, especially if the offender is your boss or a person of influence.

Societal changes and demands have long uprooted the antiquated and deep-seated belief that only men are the breadwinners and that women should be committed to the home, their husbands, and the rearing of children. Women are not weak and are not less competent than men. They are not mere sex objects. Women are entitled to equal respect and opportunity and can be great partners in building highly profitable portfolios of business and in contributing to a company's success and bottom-line profitability. Along with a business's leadership, who should be fostering the development of women for promotion to senior positions as part of their policies for company growth, victims themselves must learn how to seek opportunities, speak up for them, and properly address inappropriate behavior when it occurs. We need to get back to basics and refocus our attention on the relationships and behavior of men and women in the work environment for the better health and success of its participants and for the greater prosperity of the company.

# 8

# Responding to Bad Behavior

## Cleaning Up the Language: Have We Lost Our Ability to be Civil, Polite, and Professional?

As JR and I were pondering examples of inappropriate behavior, news and social media were exploding with bad language. When did it become OK to publicly trash-talk a woman and assume such commentary would be acceptable and without consequence? Have we, as a progressive modern society, lost our sensitivity for human decency and respect for others? What happened to our basic manners? Acting like an entitled, superior, judgmental, all-knowing, disrespectful jerk is extremely unattractive (especially if you are a woman), and none of us would appreciate being the recipient. Didn't we all learn that growing up? Remember our golden playground rule: *treat others how you want to be treated!*

Apparently, some folks do not live by this rule. If you find yourself in trouble for making a statement about another person, take a step back, and self-evaluate. Make the time to apologize, especially if you

PLAYGROUND
**RULE #2**

Treat Others
How You Want
to Be Treated

would have been offended if you had been the recipient. If you are about to send an email or make an internet post in anger, take a step back, walk around the office or grab some coffee, and then take another look before you hit send. Or, best, delete the email or post. Ask yourself how your audience will perceive the message. Ask yourself, "Is this how I would want to be treated?" This is common sense—a golden playground rule: "Treat others how you want to be treated!"

Here's an illustration. Despite all the recent news stories about Weinstein and many others who have violated women in gross numbers, the *Los Angeles Times* still allowed Pulitzer Prize–winning columnist David Horsey to post a column containing an "insensitive" description of White House press secretary Sarah Huckabee Sanders. She "does not look like the kind of woman" President Trump would choose, Horsey wrote, because he prefers "sleek beauties with long legs and stiletto heels"—Horsey imagined Trump would have picked someone more like Ivanka or Melania Trump, calling them "Barbie dolls in short, tight skirts."[1] "By comparison, Sanders looks more like a slightly chunky soccer mom who organizes snacks for the kids' games . . . Rather than the fake eyelashes and formal dresses she puts on for news briefings, Sanders seems as if she'd be more comfortable in sweats and running shoes."

Regardless of your political leanings, Sanders did not deserve such disrespectful commentary. Horsey was later forced to retract his statement and apologize, including on the November 8, 2017, episode of *Megyn Kelly Today*, in which he stated that he'd gotten caught up in the toxic political fray and lost sight of the actual impact of his post: offensive to women and ridiculously wrong. He seemed very sincere and claimed that he's always championed women and women's rights and just lost his way. Of course, Megyn Kelly didn't close the segment without letting him know that his other comments about blonde barbies at Fox in the same piece criticizing Sanders were equally inappropriate, and she named a number of female anchors at Fox who may be blonde with long legs but who are Ivy League educated (Melissa Francis and Catherine Herridge) and, in one case, a former US navy fighter pilot who fought for our country in Afghanistan (Lea Gabrielle).[2]

Men are not the only culprits using bad language. Women are violators as well. What about Roseanne Barr? In a late-night tweet on May 28, 2018, she referred to Barack Obama adviser Valerie Jarett, who is black, as "Muslim brotherhood & planet of the apes had a baby=vj." This triggered uproar and came at tremendous cost. Despite Barr's immediate apology, ABC cancelled her popular TV show, which cost Barr and all of the cast and employees of the show their jobs. "Roseanne's Twitter statement is abhorrent, repugnant and inconsistent with our values, and we have decided to cancel her show," per ABC Entertainment president Channing Dungey.[3] The show *Roseanne* had just been brought back after decades and was enjoying the end of its first season. A few days later, Samantha Bee (who often uses profanity on her political commentary show *Full Frontal with Samantha Bee*) got herself in trouble when she attacked the president's daughter, Ivanka Trump, over a photo of her hugging her small child, calling her oblivious to her dad's supposed immigration practices of separating immigrant children from their families: "You know, Ivanka, that's a beautiful photo of you and your child, but let me just say, one mother to another, do something about your dad's immigration practices you fecklss c—! . . . Put on something tight and low cut and tell your father to f—ing stop it!"[4] Bee and TBS (the network that hosts *Full Frontal*) both apologized; however, note that her show was not cancelled. Ms. Barr is an outspoken supporter of Trump, while Ms. Bee is a stark opponent of Trump. The different consequences for the entertainers were noted by conservatives.

Every day, we see instances where bad language is tolerated and often viewed lightly, including by women. Not even Trump's appalling comments caught on the infamous 2005 *Access Hollywood* tape[5] (on which he boasted about "grabbing" women "by the pussy"), his recent justification that it was just "locker room talk," or the ensuing claims by multiple women that he had sexually assaulted them prevented him from being elected president.[6] In fact, Trump later boasted that women had told him they'd heard worse and that he shouldn't worry about his comments. Some of these women were quoted on television. Trump's comments incited debate on the subject, at least, which ranged from "there should be zero tolerance" to "wake up, women, men talk trash about women all of the time" to "you (Megyn Kelly) are fascinated with sex, and you don't care about public policy."[7] Megyn was, in fact, not discussing sex but was asking Newt Gingrich whether he had any opinion on Trump's recurring disrespectful comments against women and the claims of sexual assault against him. Does Gingrich not know the difference between sex and sexual assault?

Here is a definition of sexual assault: "Sexual assault is any sexual contact or behavior that occurs without the explicit consent of the recipient. Falling under the definition of sexual assault are sexual activities as forced sexual intercourse, forcible sodomy, child molestation, incest, *fondling*, and attempted rape."[8] We have heard the saying "boys will be boys" used again and again as an excuse for men expressing their desires and dirty thoughts out loud. The *Collins English Dictionary* provides these general definitions: "If you say *boys will be boys*, for example when a group of men are behaving noisily or aggressively, you are suggesting in a light-hearted way that this is typical male behavior and will never change"; a "youthful indiscretion or exuberance [that] must be expected and tolerated."[9] We should expect the men in our lives to exercise self-control and to learn what constitutes inappropriate behavior. As a society, we should stop using the saying "boys will be boys" as an excuse or as permission for tolerating such behavior. The same goes for "locker-room talk" as an acceptable way of excusing nasty talk about women. Men, how would you feel if your mother, wife, sister, or daughter were the subject of loose talk, sexual harassment, or sexual assault? What if you, a colleague, were in an important business meeting in which an existing or a prospective client sexually harassed your female associate? Would you allow the harassing behavior to continue if she were your daughter? Where would you draw the line and speak up to stop the harassment?

It is disappointing that we have to use a sitting president as an example, but how can we not use Donald Trump? The comments he made before becoming president are notorious. Let's take the infamous comments on the 2005 *Access Hollywood* tape as an example. Our concern with Trump isn't necessarily that he made the comments as a male, although, generally, neither JR nor I have respect for any man who uses this type of language. He made these comments long before he ran for president. We both have grown a thick skin and have been around many men who can't help but be crude—even men we call colleagues, close friends, and other family members. What concerns us more is how then presidential candidate Trump responded to being called out for these comments.

Prior to Trump's presidency, he reputedly enjoyed the company of beautiful women, and if he found a woman unattractive, obstructive, or unsympathetic, he didn't hold back in publicly expressing his disdain. Many of his past comments made headlines, including his comments about Rosie O'Donnell. His most notorious rant against O'Donnell made *Entertainment Tonight* in 2006 when he said, "Rosie O'Donnell is disgusting, both inside and out. If you take a look at her, she's a slob.

How does she even get on television? If I were running *The View*, I'd fire Rosie. I'd look her right in that fat, ugly face of hers and say, 'Rosie, you're fired.' We're all a little chubby, but Rosie's just worse than most of us. But it's not the chubbiness—Rosie is a very unattractive person, both inside and out."

What about Hillary Clinton? In a tweet on April 16, 2015, Trump said, "If Hillary Clinton can't satisfy her husband, what makes her think that she can satisfy America @realDonaldTrump#2016president"—a tweet that, according to theory, appeared to reference Bill Clinton's affair with Monica Lewinsky. Then came his attacks on Megyn Kelly. After the debate on August 8, 2015, and after calling her a "bimbo" on Twitter, Trump suggested in a CNN interview that her questioning was a result of her menstruating: "You could see there was blood coming out of her eyes. Blood was coming out of her wherever." Trump later denied this was his intention. Carly Fiorina was next. On September 9, 2015, according to *Rolling Stone* magazine, Trump said, "Look at that face. Would anyone vote for that?" Trump made many more comments.[10]

When the *Access Hollywood* tape leaked, Trump should have immediately apologized with sincerity for any inappropriate behavior, emphasized that he's changed over the years, and made clear he's not proud of his past behavior and that he's a different man today. Of course, that's assuming these statements would have been truthful. After all, he has two beautiful, well-educated daughters whom we believe he respects. He's also married to a strong, intelligent woman who would not likely appreciate him misbehaving today, although recent news of alleged affairs in 2006 and 2007 with porn star Stormy Daniels and 1998 *Playboy* Playmate of the Year Karen McDougal must be troubling to Melania. Both of these women are looking to invalidate confidentiality agreements and speak publicly about their affairs with Trump. Had he acknowledged his behavior when the *Access Hollywood* tape leaked and shown some level of sincere remorse, he might have been believable, and he might have strengthened his credibility. Instead, he was upset that he had been taped without his knowledge and tried to excuse his comments as "locker-room" talk, implying that this type of talk in a locker-room setting is common and acceptable—sparking yet more controversy. Trump eventually offered an apology for the crude comments that had been caught on tape, including to his family, but his effort wasn't viewed as sincere by many. He also denied ever "following through" with his comments and engaging in any inappropriate behavior, which inspired several women to come forward with claims of sexual assault going back to the 1980s (all of which Trump has denied).[11]

Our point is that no matter how offensive Trump's comments and actions might have been, they didn't stop Trump from becoming president. Women still voted for him, either because they believed this behavior is standard for men and they accept it or because they believed Trump's campaign promises far outweighed any character flaws. We believe it was the former.

Although Trump's behavior was unbecoming of a gentleman and has certainly raised serious doubts about his integrity, this behavior did not seem to matter much—not just for Trump but for many men. After all, Trump isn't the first elected official to have behaved badly toward women. Many past presidents were unfaithful to their wives, like Bill Clinton and John F. Kennedy, to name a few.[12] As Bill Clinton recently proved in an interview with NBC's Craig Melvin, he fails to fully appreciate his past actions (specifically those involving Monica Lewinsky and the abuse of the power relationship he had with her as a president versus an intern) as sexual harassment, stating: "Nobody believes that I got out of that for free. I left the White House $16 million in debt . . . This was litigated 20 years ago. Two-thirds of the American people sided with me and they were not insensitive to that." In light of the #MeToo movement, his comments defending his actions and noting that he had been victimized instead of apologizing—he apologized to Ms. Lewinsky publicly, but not in person—raised eyebrows among members of his own party and renewed discussion of his apparent lack of remorse and lack of understanding that he had done anything wrong. While Clinton praised the #MeToo movement as "way overdue," he added, "It doesn't mean I agree with everything."[13]

Regardless, *nothing* excuses disrespectful behavior and language toward a woman. Especially by a woman to a woman. Consider the following quotes, which we find very compelling.

"Integrity is choosing your thoughts and actions
based on values rather than personal gain."
—Chris Karcher

"Character isn't something you were born with and can't
change, like your fingerprints. It's something you weren't
born with and must take responsibility for forming."
—Jim Rohn

We must make every effort to behave with civility, compassion, and respect. Remind your fellow colleagues, friends, and family to do the same, and teach your children accordingly.

## Learning to Take Control Immediately and Modify Behavior

Our focus in this book is to help our readers address inappropriate behavior in real time. We believe that, in many cases, it may take only a simple "redirect" or gentle "reprimand" by the affected person or by a witness to resolve a perpetrator's behavior at the time of the harassment. Doing so with humor will often resolve the situation. It's not realistic to think that complaining to the boss, to a more senior colleague, or to HR will immediately address and resolve the harassment. Those affected are typically afraid of potentially generating adverse publicity, tainting their reputations within the company, and compromising their careers. In many cases, the boss or senior person is the perpetrator, the person being asked for help may not appreciate the severity of the behavior or know how to address it, or there is no HR department or experienced person who can handle the complaint. In most situations, it's much more productive to learn how to draw a line of respect in a firm but gentle manner—again, with a little bit of humor if possible. Using an applicable playground rule might help with the communication. If you're too aggressive or insulting, you'll put that person on the defensive, and they'll miss the point of your address. Future communications will be awkward, and you may have created an adversary concerning your future career. If you address the harassment immediately, you might ease communications in the working relationship going forward, which includes preserving potential business for the company if the bad behavior is by an outside vendor or client.

Of course, if your actions don't resolve the situation, a more aggressive response is necessary. Let's talk about another example. Julie just started her job with a small real-estate company. It didn't take long for her to be sexually harassed at a client entertainment event her company was hosting at a hockey game. At the event, Julie tried to converse with a client about her company and future joint business opportunities, but the client was more interested in encouraging an intimate relationship by putting his hand on her leg and trying to feel up her skirt. When Julie told her male superiors, their reaction was disbelief—no way the client would behave in such a fashion. She had to convince them to watch the client at the next several encounters. To make matters worse, she was harassed by other vendors and clients as well. According to her accounts, this was a new revelation for her male superiors. She is one of few women at her company and one of the first to complain about sexual harassment.

Entertaining vendors and clients outside the office is not an invitation to take advantage of young associates, yet some vendors and clients have a different impression regarding what "after hours enter-tainment" means. Her boss should put a stop to the behavior at the next customer event, in a lighthearted tone of voice. "Tyrant Ivan, our associates are not here to entertain you. They are here to help educate you on our company's products. Let her do her job!" Or, "Tyrant Ivan, hands off, and no touching! You will get us all in trouble with HR. She is here to tell you about the company!" Tyrant Ivan will listen to the superior, whether man or woman. As for the young associate, she could gently remove his hand with a smile and say, "Tyrant Ivan, we are not permitted to fraternize with customers or clients. You will get us in a lot of trouble! Let's go talk to some of the other folks." Remind him of the rule he may have learned on his playground: "Respect the playground and its players!" Then get up, and join others. If the violator does not stop, find a more senior person, and ask for help.

Until her company implements a sexual harassment policy, as well as procedures for filing complaints, and appropriately educates its employees (including senior personnel) on appropriate conduct, the young female associate and her male colleagues will need guidance on how to deal with this type of bad behavior when they encounter it. Dealing with this issue quickly and effectively will help foster respect and preserve careers.

It is up to us women—and our male counterparts who understand the issue of sexual harassment—to take on a more significant role in educating our colleagues, friends, and families about how to handle situations more appropriately, thus fostering confidence and a healthier work environment.

Coming back to Trump, the woman who supposedly told Trump that she "had heard worse comments" and he needn't worry about them could instead have told him, "I am a big supporter of you, Mr. Trump; however, what you said was not appropriate, and you have to promise that you will remove that kind of bad talk about women from your vocabulary!" Would that have been so difficult? Certainly she didn't appreciate the meaning of what she'd said, and if she did, what message is she sending to younger women and men in her family and her social circles? With respect to the young female actress Arianne Zucker, who was directed by Billy Bush to hug Trump after he exited the bus and uttered the words on the infamous *Hollywood Access* tape, if she felt uncomfortable with the request to hug Trump, she could've simply smiled, extended her hand or patted him on the back, and said, "No hugs on set!" She could also have said, "Hugs are not part of my job description!" or, "I am flattered at the suggestion, but hugs are not my thing!" A lighthearted or humorous but firm response is best. Billy Bush might then have known not to suggest she hug someone again. Note that Billy Bush's involvement cost him his job on *The Today Show* on NBC.[14]

Remember the young associate who found out that her hotel room was adjacent to her boss's? She should have asked the clerk to move her hotel room to a different floor and then told her boss that she had to change rooms because the hotel had inadvertently put them next to each other. Her explanation could be that she didn't want there to be any appearance of impropriety and that she had done it to protect both of their reputations. She could have reminded him of this playground rule: "Respect the playground and its players!" He would undoubtedly have received the message not to try to invite her to his room. If he'd invited her anyway, she could have said, in a lighthearted tone of voice, "Thanks for the offer, but going to your room would make me uncomfortable. I don't want either of us to get into trouble. Let's compare notes in the lobby bar or tomorrow at breakfast." Then she could have walked away.

We understand it's difficult to respond immediately and to say the right thing, but do your best to keep your response light and innocent (as opposed to accusatory)—at least at first. When Bill O'Reilly allegedly told a woman to come to his room after dinner, which she politely declined, he supposedly became defensive and said, "What do you mean? You think I am going to attack you or something?" According to the woman's account, O'Reilly later retaliated against her professionally for rejecting him.[15] One of her options might have been to laugh and say, "Yes, Bill, I do think you will take advantage of me. You do have that reputation!" If she would have then walked away, maybe he wouldn't have been offended and might have left her alone. Finding the right words is difficult, but try not to put the violator on the defensive in your initial communications. If you put them on the defensive, they may not hear what you have to say and—more likely—may be occupied with how to get back at you. Be gentle and humorous, and get away from the situation. If that does not work, then go to Plan B, and *take a more aggressive approach.*

I remember a situation in which, at a company meeting out of town, a colleague from another city followed me to my hotel room after drinks at the bar with a larger group of colleagues and started banging on my door. I could tell at the bar that he was interested in me, so I'd found an excuse to leave and had gone back to my hotel room. I went to the door and, without opening it, told him I was on a call with my husband and asked whether I could talk to him in the morning. It took him a few minutes, but he eventually left. What if you are out of town at a dinner hosted by your company? Say a potential client attending the dinner is not listening to your pitch for business; instead, he's making comments about taking you out later and maybe going to your hotel room. You could gently stop him and say, "Thanks for the offer, but we are here for business. May I please continue?" If you are caught off guard, your supervisor should step in and say, "Glad you like my colleague, but that is not the purpose of our dinner meeting. We are here to make a pitch! May she please continue?"

Say you are in a strategy meeting at a client's office early one Saturday morning. You are the only woman in attendance, and you are the most junior in rank. The meeting is just about to start when a woman dressed in her tennis outfit comes in to check on the group. The president of the company looks pleased and says something like, "Nice outfit, Susan! Why don't you give us all a twirl so we can get a good look!" To your surprise, she obliges. He is her big boss, and our guess is that she didn't think she had a choice other than to comply with his request. She could have laughed at him, said, "You don't pay me enough to do that!" and then turned around and left. What would you have done in her shoes?

Let's talk about a few situations that may not necessarily involve bad intent. JR recalls a time when she was on a flight with a client to visit a property. After several hours of conversation while sitting next to her on the plane, her client suddenly reached around and kissed her forcefully. Surprised, she gently pushed him back into his chair and told him that although she was flattered by his attention, she was not interested in a personal relationship and wanted to keep things professional. She said it in a lighthearted tone of voice and then continued on with their conversation as if nothing had happened. He seemed embarrassed at first and apologized immediately, but he told her later that he appreciated her not making him feel terrible or uncomfortable about his advance. In JR's opinion, the client had a crush on her and was not necessarily seeking to abuse their relationship.

One day at my job, I met up with a group of men for lunch in the lobby. As we were waiting, huddled in a group, I was catching up a senior attorney on a matter we were handling together. He appeared to be listening but was staring square at my boobs (which were fully covered). Instinctually, I raised both hands with my fingers pointed at his eyes, motioning for him to raise his eyes to mine, and said in a gentle but lighthearted voice, "Buck"—not his real name—"my eyes are up here!" There were a few laughs from the group, and I could tell he was embarrassed, but I continued with my report as if I was not bothered by the incident. I knew his behavior was a momentary lapse in judgment without any malicious or deviant intent. The same incident with the same attorney happened several more times, but all I had to do was motion with my hands and he'd immediately adjust his eyes. Before too long, he was not doing that anymore—hopefully not to any woman. I had modified his behavior.

For now, it is evident from the #MeToo movement that lewd comments and unwanted sexual advances are alive and well and that they continue to be tolerated and excused within and without the workplace. Although most companies have policies and procedures to deal with sexual harassment complaints, we know the consequences to the complainant can be dire, including severe mental distress, loss of confidence, retaliation, and loss of employment. In many cases, it may not be realistic, possible, or smart to file a complaint. The behavior may be repetitive and perpetrated by several violators on many different occasions; it may be committed by your boss or by an outside vendor or customer whom your company does not control. Men and women alike experience disrespectful behavior toward colleagues in their presence, and in those types of situations, they're often unsure how to react and what to say. Given the frequency of these occurrences, it is not realistic to expect to resolve the behavior with a visit to HR each and every time. The objectionable behavior must be dealt with immediately, at the time of the occurrence or soon thereafter. Women in the workforce and their male counterparts, colleagues, and superiors need to be better prepared to deal with these situations as they occur and to immediately educate perpetrators when they cross the line. If we can respond immediately and appropriately, drawing a firm line of what is acceptable, we might be able to modify behavior without having to take more serious action, such as filing a complaint, which could potentially ruin the reputation or career of the victim. The goal is to arm men and women with commonsense tools for stopping bad behavior in its tracks with confidence and creating a better and healthier Sandbox.

## Using the Boys' Club to Your Advantage

What if you are in a staff meeting with all men, and they keep commenting on a female colleague's body parts each time she comes in the room? Or perhaps they are rating her on a scale of one to ten and then laughing about each other's comments. Tolerating the bad behavior or remaining silent may signal your approval, and the men in the room are likely to continue acting badly. If you decide to speak up, however, what you say and how you say it might make a difference in your career and in your future relationships with your male coworkers. They may decide that you are no longer part of their group meetings or social interactions, such as group lunches or happy hour—no longer part of the "boys' club." If you are one of the few women in your office or in your industry, you may care about the boys' club. This club is where deals are dissected and discussed, strategies are explored, and solutions are pondered. As a woman, you can learn a lot about how men think, strategize, and work through problems. If you are engaged by the men and they respect you and value your input, they will support you, incorporate you into their business world, and help with your career. Ideally, a woman looking to grow and progress in her job should not have to worry about the boys' club. However, if you are working in a male-dominated environment, dealing with the boys' club may be your reality. Learning from your male colleagues is important. First, they will need to trust you. This does not mean that you have to sacrifice your values, submit to or tolerate sexual harassment, or "play along" with their banter in order to be considered part of their inner circle. We will explore this subject further in our next book.

You have several options. You could simply listen, take notes, and then turn them in to HR, risking that they'll find out about your involvement and exclude you going forward because they no longer consider you trustworthy. You could be confrontational and say with a raised or stern voice, "Stop talking about her like that. You are making me uncomfortable!" Many experts believe this is the best way to combat sexual harassment since it catches the perpetrator off guard and challenges his manhood, status, and prestige, especially if you are admonishing him in front of an audience. However, this type of approach is likely to put the violator on the defensive, and you may have created an enemy. Generally speaking, men may not respect men who are called out by a woman. We agree that certain situations require confrontation, especially if you are encountering repeated or uncomfortable behavior of sexual harassment. Know, however, that you are likely to risk an icy or defensive response and may be disliked and excluded from the boys' club going forward.

Initally, consider a more gentle but firm approach that gets their attention but leaves their egos intact, especially if the perpetrator is among a group. The goal is to communicate that they've misbehaved but are being offered an opportunity to fix the behavior going forward in a positive manner without any repercussions. They may appreciate that you are trying to help them and keep them out of trouble. This approach is more likely to foster trust. For example, stand up (to get their attention), smile, and say with a firm but gentle voice, "Now, now, gentlemen. Simmer down. You are disrespectful. If she were your sister or daughter, you would not want guys making those comments about her, would you? What would your mom say if she heard your comments? Let's be respectful to your female colleagues going forward." You could add, "If someone hears you, you could be subject to sexual harassment claims!" The idea is to draw a firm line and create a boundary of respect every single time you're exposed to sexual harassment. If the behavior occurs again, remind them of your prior warning. Remind them that you are looking out for their well-being. Use the applicable playground rules to help communicate the innapropriate behavior, such as, "Respect the playground and its players! Treat others how you want to be treated!"

Audrey Nelson said it well in a recent article: "The good ol' boys club needs to know when it crosses the line. Set boundaries and address issues from a position of strength, not weakness. Don't say what they did wrong (whining and negative); say what you want them to do (positive)."[16] In this context, another playground rule you can use regarding treatment of colleagues comes to mind: "Use nice words, be polite, and have good manners."

We believe a gentle but firm or humorous approach is the best way to generate respect from your male counterparts and superiors. Recently, someone said, "This approach is not healthy. Women should be able to be themselves, not a humorous version of themselves!" Again, JR and I are recommending this approach based on our own experiences in very male-dominated environments. You have to be able, for example, to walk into a room filled with men and make them comfortable that you are the proper person with the leading expertise to handle their work project. You have to be able to build trust and confidence the very moment you take that first phone call or have that first face-to-face meeting and in every interaction thereafter. You

PLAYGROUND
RULE #4

Use Nice Words,
Be Polite, and
Have Good
Manners

have to command attention and respect as a female leader throughout your relationship with your colleagues, customers, and clients. If you put the violator on the defensive coming out of the gate, you will not be able to foster a good long-term relationship. Be gentle but firm, and if you can, handle the violator with a little humor. If you can modify his behavior at the beginning of your relationship (with an occasional reminder if needed), you may have a supporter in the long term. He may come back as a client or refer your business, and if he is your colleague, he will want to work with you on future transactions.

In our experience, being defensive or bitchy is not helpful. If you handle your objections or admonishments with a firm but humorous tone, you are more likely to get their attention without putting them on the defensive. The men may be less likely to exclude you from important meetings and social situations if they see that you are confident and can handle them without negative consequences. They will be more relaxed and inclusive knowing that if they act poorly, you will not hesitate to put them in their place instead of ratting them out to HR. Professor of literature Regina Barreca says women in higher-level positions must use humor because it "appears as evidence of intelligence, personal strength, and quick thinking."[17]

As the male, if you are in a group or are a bystander, you have an excellent opportunity to exhibit your leadership skills and manipulate the behavior. Men will listen to men. A simple, "Hey, gentlemen, stop the commentary! Not cool!"—with subsequent reminders, if needed—will go a long way toward setting a positive tone for behavior going forward. Men, your female colleagues need your help!

**COMPANY PLAYGROUND RULE #2**

Remind Others of the Rules; Don't Be a Bystander

In summary, remember the following playground rule: "Remind others of the rules; don't be a bystander!"

## Don't Be a Bystander

What if you are outside the office, and the bad behavior involves a person who does not work for the company? Men, imagine a situation where you are the boss or a senior executive of a company and are attending a business meeting to sell a new product. You are present with a young female associate, who is the expert regarding the product. The potential client is not focused on the presentation; rather, he is making remarks about how he would prefer to take your associate out for drinks and then later see what she has under her clothes. You know this potential client is important to the company and that getting the business would be very profitable. If she reacts in a confrontational manner to put this person in his place, she risks a defensive or other adverse reaction. Say she says, "Sir, your comments are making me uncomfortable. May I please continue with the benefits of our product?" Although she may have his attention, he may not necessarily like her confrontation. Her comments might hurt his ego, and he will be thinking about how to get back at her instead of listening to her presentation.

You may think, *I would cut the meeting short and walk away. Why deal with creeps?* JR and I both agree with your thought; however, this is not necessarily realistic. What if your company needs the business? What if the young associate wants to develop a business relationship with the potential client? Yes, there are too many creeps in the world, but there will be times when you are required to interact with them for business purposes. The business opportunity may be worthy of trying to modify the violator's behavior. The young associate could respond with humor: "I'm flattered, but I may get fired for even considering your invitation. Best to stick to the purpose of this meeting!" Maybe he will be comfortable with her response.

As a bystander, consider aiding your colleague by putting the potential client in his place, allowing her to continue without any damage to the potential relationship going forward. Disarm him so he is forced to abandon his quest and has no choice but to reengage with the purpose of the meeting. If you're the direct supervisor, it is important for you to chime in. Maybe you could say, "Hey, Insecure Joe. I know she is a lovely young lady, but we do not allow our employees to fraternize with customers. Can you please let her continue? She is the expert, and you want to hear what she has to say about this product!" The potential client may get the message and hopefully treat the young associate with respect going forward. Remember the playground rule: "Respect the playground and its players!"

What if you are in a similar meeting, and the potential client will not make eye contact with your female associate? Instead, he directs his comments and questions to you, as the male superior, even though your associate is the specialist regarding your product. In many cases, men are not interested in doing business with women, are disrespectful toward women, or do not want to deal with nonsenior women and would rather deal with men. JR and I have also seen situations in which a female directs her attention solely to the men in the room and ignores the other females present. Whether male or female, it is possible the violator wants to drain any confidence your associate has by addressing all questions to the other gender in the room. By ignoring her, he or she intends to throw her off balance and to make it difficult for her to complete her presentation. In this situation, it is imperative that you, as the supervisor, direct the violator's attention to your associate as the person with the requisite knowledge. You may have to do this multiple times, but eventually, the potential client will realize that you respect your female colleague's expertise and that directing attention to the supervisor will not get their questions answered.

If you, as supervisor, do not help direct the violator, your associate could gently insert herself by forcing attention back to her. She could put her hand on your arm and ask, "Would you mind if I answer this question, since I have all of the relevant information?" She should then look directly at the potential client and respond to the question confidently and calmly. She should repeat if necessary. In some cases, once you add value to the conversation and the potential client experiences you as the expert or the person with the knowledge, he or she will be more comfortable working with you directly. Business dealings often involve difficult people, even creeps. It is not realistic to believe that you can avoid them or choose not to do business with them without losing business. In many cases, with a little effort, you can modify behavior for a better future relationship.

# 9

# As a Society, What Positive Changes Can We Implement?

## Changes in Law

As a result of the #MeToo movement, a number of changes to the law are being contemplated or should be considered, including the following.

### 1. Nondisclosure Agreements

Remove mandatory nondisclosure and confidentiality provisions involving sexual harassment claims (and block courts from enforcing such provisions). Barring secrecy would allow predators to be held accountable and would likely discourage them from repeating bad behavior. These types of provisions are used by employers to force silence, protecting the company's reputation and bottom line.

### 2. Forced Arbitration Provisions

Remove forced arbitration agreements involving sexual harassment and discrimination claims (and block courts from enforcing such provisions).

These agreements are often required as a condition to employment and eliminate the Seventh Amendment right to a jury trial. Employers use these types of agreements to handle workplace disputes internally, avoiding the courts and the high cost of potentially protracted litigation. A bipartisan group of lawmakers—including senators Kirstin Gillibrand of New York and Lindsey Graham of South Carolina, with the assistance of Gretchen Carlson—have introduced a bill for a federal law to end forced arbitration for harassment and gender discrimination, which keeps some sixty million Americans from being able to use the courts to settle cases. The attorneys general of every American state and every US territory have banded together to support this effort.[1]

### 3. Statute of Limitations

Extend or eliminate statutes of limitations for sexual misconduct or assault cases. Current time periods vary from state to state and appear to be arbitrary. Connecticut, for example, has a five-year statute of limitations (subject to certain exceptions), while, last year, California became the seventeenth state to eliminate statute of limitations periods for such crimes. The issue regarding statutes of limitations is controversial. Statute of limitations periods are intended to exact a toll on justice by allowing victims proper time to process their traumatic experiences and to file claims, but they are also intended to protect a defendant against stale claims after a certain period of time, within which a diligent person would have accused the defendant. Memories and details fade, and witnesses may disappear, risking wrongful conviction or unfair prosecution.[2]

### 4. Require Company Reporting

Regular reporting requirements regarding the number of sexual harassment claims filed, settlement amounts, and corrective actions taken would foster accountability and transparency, helping deter bad behavior.

## 5. Lawsuits under Title VII of the Civil Rights Act of 1964[3]

Title VII should be amended to hold that individual harassers may be sued, not just the corporate employer. If harassers see their own careers, houses, and assets on the line in litigation, that may be a more powerful deterrent than all of the talk shows and corporate sensitivity training combined.

## 6. Title VII and the Fifteen-Employee Requirement

Change Title VII of the Civil Rights Act of 1964 to eliminate the fifteen-employee threshold and include all working people, regardless of field or employment classification.

## 7. Legislate a 30 Percent Quota

Legislate a required percentage quota for women in leadership positions. According to some surveys, 30 percent is the magic number—"the tipping point at which women stop being a beleaguered minority—tokens, unable to change organizational culture—and serve as effective change agents."[4]

## 8. New Tax Cuts and Jobs Act

The Tax Cuts and Jobs Act recently passed by Congress limits the deductions that businesses may take for attorney's fees or payments of sexual harassment settlements. Under the act, "no deduction shall be allowed . . . for (1) any settlement or payment related to sexual harassment or sexual abuse *if such settlement or payment is subject to a nondisclosure agreement*, or (2) attorney's fees related to such a settlement or payment" (emphasis ours). This new act will hopefully encourage companies to become more diligent in policing sexual harassment behavior and to eliminate the use of nondisclosure agreements in such situations.

# Nonlegal Actions

It will take time for the laws to improve with respect to sexual harassment. Until that time, effect changes that make a difference.

## 1. Making Controversial Contract Provisions Optional

Until the law changes, companies could make "forced arbitration" and "nondisclosure agreements" optional. For example, on December 19, 2017, Microsoft announced that it was ending its requirement for forced arbitration agreements with employees who make sexual harassment claims.[5] Uber has followed suit, deciding that it will no longer require its users or drivers to go through arbitration if they are claiming assault or harassment. Nor will it require them to sign nondisclosure agreements. They have also agreed to be transparent about sexual assault data.[6]

## 2. Publishing Company Efforts to Set an Example

Publishing your sexual harassment policy gives notice to the public that you are taking the issue of sexual harassment seriously and invites commentary regarding any needed improvements. Setting an example might cause others to follow suit. Facebook, for example, has posted its sexual harassment policy publicly.[7] New York City has enacted one of the most expansive packages of workplace anti-sexual-harassment laws in the nation, applicable to all New York City workers in the public and private sectors, even those working for small employers with fewer than five employees.[8] The legislation includes a prohibition against nondisclosure and mandatory arbitration clauses in sexual harassment cases and requires all companies to enact written antiharassment policies and annual training effective October 9, 2018.[9]

## 3. Rally the Troops

After experiencing years of sexual harassment with little to no corrective action after complaining to HR, a group of women inside Nike's

Beaverton, Oregon, headquarters had finally had enough and started a small revolt. Their complaints included gender discrimination, disrespect at group meetings, exclusion from advancement in certain divisions, exclusion of women from the inner circle of male decision makers, and lack of female leadership. After surveying their female peers, the results, in the form of completed questionnaires, landed on the desk of the company's CEO. The result? A series of departures of male executives, including the president of the Nike brand, Trevor Edwards, and his lieutenant, Jayme Martin, who ran Nike's global business.[10]

## 4. Social Media and Campaigns

Social media campaigns and movements can influence action taken against alleged perpetrators of sexual harassment and assault.

> **a. #MuteRKelly Movement:** This current movement seeks to hold R. Kelly accountable for his alleged sexual misconduct against black girls and women, urging artists, radio stations, record companies, streaming platforms, and concert venues to cut ties with the alleged predator.[11]

> **b. Time's Up Campaign:** The Women of Color committee within Time's Up has demanded appropriate investigations and inquiries into the allegations of R. Kelly's alleged abuse, which have been made by women and their families for more than two decades and include allegations of sexual coercion, leading a sex cult, and physical abuse.[12]

## 5. Discourage Vulgarity in Language

Loose language promotes a negative culture. Discourage such language from the top down, and set an example and precedent. Women, don't join in the coarse language. Such language will not make you equal to men or gain their respect. Knowing and doing your job well will gain you the respect of your fellow colleagues.

## 6.  Do Not Support Harassers

Many universities are revoking honorary degrees given to alleged sexual harassers, including University of Pennsylvania's honorary degrees to Bill Cosby and Steve Wynn.[13] Cosby received his honorary degree in 1990, and Wynn received his in 2006.

## 7.  Teach Consent Early

Talk to your kids regularly about sexual harassment, assault, and how important it is that your body not be violated by anyone. Teach them that they are "the boss of their body" and that, unless they have consented, no one is permitted to touch them. Teach your son that consent requires a yes and that "enthusiastic" consent is best so that he doesn't misinterpret her communication.

# 10

# Takeaways for Women in the Sandbox

### 1. Don't Be One of the Boys

Be careful. Being one of the boys has some associated risks. You may think that staying silent or laughing at bad male behavior about women and their bodies may result in greater respect for you as a female colleague. Maybe it will make the men think you are tough and strong and get you invited to activities with the male "inner circle," such as meetings, lunches, and happy hours. If you tolerate their bad behavior and don't take action to correct it, however, who knows what they are saying behind your back? Condoning their behavior will only encourage them to continue.

### 2. Pick Your Battles

If you work in a male-dominated environment, you are likely to be exposed to constant male banter and teasing. This behavior is often meant to be funny or competitive and not intended as a personal insult. Don't hesitate to dish it back, but try to stay out of the gutter. Remain professional and calm, if you can. If the banter and teasing is repetitive or particularly offensive, address the behavior using Plan A and the rules of the playground. Your male colleagues will learn not to push you around.

### 3. Draw a Hard Line

If you find yourself exposed to inappropriate and sexist comments and behavior, don't hesitate to shut the violators down firmly but gently. We believe it is better not to put the men on the defensive. Use a little humor, at least the first time. You could laugh and say gently, "Guys, seriously, did you just hear yourselves? Your comments are inappropriate! What would your mothers think?" If it happens at work, you can even add, "If you are overheard, you could be subject to sexual harassment claims!" If someone touches you inappropriately, remove the offender's hand, back away, or get up and create distance. Look the violator in the eye, and gently tell him or her, "Hey! I am not available for touching!" If someone is standing too close to you or is leaning over your shoulder and maybe looking down your cleavage, say, "Hey! Please back away—you are too close for comfort!" Our favorite: "Beep beep, back up that truck! You're in my space!" If the violator has done it before or is insistent, be more forceful. Say, "Please stop touching me!" or, "Please back away!" and, "You are making me uncomfortable!" Stand up, if necessary, to emphasize your point.

Learn how to draw a firm line and create a boundary of respect. Use the playground rules to help with your communications. "Respect the playground and its players! Treat others how you want to be treated! Inappropriate treatment of players is strictly prohibited!" Do it every single time you are exposed to sexual harassment. Be consistent. It is the best way to generate respect and trust from your colleagues and superiors. If you take action immediately, gently, and with a little humor, your colleagues will be more amenable to your admonishment and are more likely to listen and respect your position. They'll be more relaxed around you knowing that if they act badly, you will put them in their place instead of running to HR.

### 4. Don't Be Afraid to Share Your Opinion

Don't be afraid to speak up and share your thoughts, especially if you are subject to or witness sexual harassment. Be gentle but firm. Express your concern in a nonthreatening way to avoid putting the other person on the defensive. If you're in a meeting and would like to contribute, but someone is ignoring you, is not letting you speak, or is interrupting you, stand up, if necessary, so you can't be refused. Be prepared regarding the subject matter. Knowledge is power.

### 5. Don't Be Your Assistant

When you are around clients or men, avoid tasks that are appropriately the responsibility of a less senior staff member, assistant, or secretary (such as making copies or fetching coffee). If you are asked to "go fetch," be kind, and advise the asker that you will have a more appropriate person handle it. Then pick up the phone and coordinate the task, or ask your assistant to enter the room, introduce him or her, and make that person available for any such requests. If you work for a company and don't have an assistant or secretary, solicit the assistance of another appropriate person to handle these tasks, such as the receptionist, a clerk in the mail room, or another member of the staff.

### 6. Don't Give Anyone a Reason to Challenge Your Abilities; Be Prepared

A superior once welcomed me to his team as the only female, but he noted, "This team works hard, including late at night and on the weekends, so you will have to buck up, since women can't perform like men."

I smiled and said, "Thank you for your confidence, sir, and I look forward to proving you wrong!" And I did. I made sure my work was top quality, and I went the extra mile. For years, after projects had been completed and he'd complimented my work, I would make comments like, "Not bad for a woman, huh?" and he would laugh, remembering our first meeting. I agree with Megyn Kelly's view on this subject in her book *Settle For More*. "It's not that I reject the idea of demanding a place at the table—quite the contrary. But in my own experience, the most effective way to get opportunities is with performance, not persistence. Hard work matters. I really believe that."[1] I grew up in a military family, in which I was taught that if I worked hard to achieve to the best of my abilities with poise and confidence, my work, attitude, and dedication would be noticed and rewarded. I was taught to never give anyone a reason to criticize my work or my abilities and to show that I was adding value to the task, the team, the client, and the company. JR was raised with similar values. She grew up in a fourth-generation ranching and farming family and was taught to work hard and to stand by her word. If you are not recognized for your contributions despite such a work ethic, you can demand to be acknowledged. Your superiors will be hard pressed not to give you a seat at the table.

## 7. Don't Date a Colleague

I was recently asked in a symposium whether it was OK to date a colleague. I stopped in my tracks and was surprised anyone would even ask that question. Relationships at work are risky and can put both parties in a difficult position, especially if the male is a superior. What if the relationship began as an affair? How would that impact the career of the female? Who do you think would have to leave the job if the company had an antidating or antinepotism policy? Whether or not there is such a policy, if you date a colleague, matters become complicated if you break up. Why put yourself through the drama of possibly being fired or, after a breakup, suffering through the aftermath where both of you work? Just don't do it.

## 8. Dress Professionally; Don't Be A Distraction

Make a conscious effort to present yourself in a professional manner. Plain and elegant is better than tight clothes that show cleavage and too much skin. Stay away from loud perfume. Aim for grace, dignity, and calm. Be an elegant contributor, not a distraction. My mother always told me that how you dress and how you maintain your hair, nails, and toes reflects who you are as a person. If you look disheveled, unclean, or disorganized, your audience may be concerned about how you might handle their project. The same goes for the state of your office and the presentation of any work product. Of course, how you dress is your own personal choice; however, if you look professional in a style that makes you comfortable, you are likely to exude and engender confidence. Ask for help at your favorite stores if you need fashion assistance. You don't have to spend a fortune. Expensive name brands won't make you any more successful. How you look and feel will help improve your outlook as you approach the rest of your day, including your job, and will likely build your confidence!

## 9. Be Confident, but Don't Be a Bitch

Don't play the tough girl, charging in with aggressive behavior like you have something to prove. Don't use foul language, and don't demean and discredit others. It won't earn you respect, and you will be viewed with suspicion. Be firm, but gentle, not loud. Be confident. Play to your own strengths and qualities. My mom said it best: "You have the one weapon men don't have. You are a woman. Something a man can't help pay attention to and something they need to survive. It is a gentle but powerful weapon. Use your qualities to your advantage."

## 10. Monitor Your Emotions

If a situation is making you angry or upset and you find that you are about to get emotional, excuse yourself, and regroup. You do not want to lose control and give another person the satisfaction of having upset you. That person will find a way to use your reaction to their advantage and portray you as whiny or weak. It's OK to say, "Excuse me, I will be right back." If you do happen to cry, don't fret. Be honest, and say, "I didn't mean to cry. I have had a tough day, and this topic makes me emotional. Let me regroup, and we can talk later." You may appear stronger and more in control if you own up to your emotions. If you appear weak and whiny, you may be less likely to be taken seriously.

## 11. Who Are Your Allies?

Some of our very best friends are men we met through work. If we faced sexual harassment or other difficult situations, they would be the first to assist. Get to know your male colleagues, and make friends. Turn them into your allies. You might need them some day.

# Conclusion

My twenty-one-year-old daughter, Nicole, asked my husband recently, "If there are three equally qualified candidates, and one is a woman, who would you think a company would pick for the job?"

He thought for a moment, then responded, "Well, back in the day, hiring considerations were different. They might have been concerned about her status. Was she married or going to have children? If yes, it might compromise her ability to travel and work late hours. It might add a level of stress that could affect her being able to perform to the best of her abilities. She would have to be extraordinary to get the job. I'm not sure those considerations have changed."

My daughter was concerned. "But Dad, that is not fair. She likely worked very hard for the opportunity, and today, that would be discrimination and illegal according to hiring laws."

"Agreed," my husband responded. "However, back then, that was reality. Today, although the laws have changed, these questions might still be in the employer's mind—subconsciously."

My daughter was not deterred. "What if your daughter were the candidate? Would you be OK with that type of discrimination? Would you not want me to have equal opportunity? What about when Mom started her legal career?"

He pondered. Of course, somehow his wife and daughters were different. They deserved equal opportunity.

Not too long ago, I was at lunch with a group of my husband's old work friends. One of them brought his daughter, a college senior. We were deep in discussion about the job market and where she might want to work when one of the guys offered her an interview at his company, a large real-estate firm. The opportunity was square within her interests. Her father leaned over to her and said, "This company is very male dominated. If you were the lucky candidate to get that job, you would have to be prepared to deal with discrimination and sexual harassment. Lots of male banter and sexual innuendo."

I turned to the potential employer and asked whether the company had any policies against that type of behavior. He responded as expected: "Of course we do." Then came the lengthy discussion about the reality of enforcement and the importance of learning how to stop that type of behavior in its tracks when it occurs. Working in this male-dominated environment would not be without its challenges.

My older daughter, Samantha, was born a sports fanatic and has no trouble competing with any male in terms of sports knowledge. During her senior year in high school, we thought she might pursue a career as a sports announcer. When she started considering job options, Samantha announced that she would not put herself in that type of male-dominated environment by taking on such a position. It would not be worth how she would be treated. It broke my heart, since I knew that sports were her passion and that she was tough enough to handle that environment.

Choosing a career path is a big decision, and a career in a heavily male-dominated environment can make the decision more daunting. If you are bold enough to apply for the job, then you have to overcome the prejudices and unconscious biases that might exist during the interview process. If you get the job, then you have to learn how to survive bullying, sexual harassment, and discrimination, as well as how to keep your job—you, the intelligent, ambitious, eager-to-impress, idealistic new employee. As we've noted, not much has changed regarding the equal treatment of genders. Given the frequency with which sexual harassment and discrimination occur in the workplace, we must embolden women (and men) to call out bad behavior. We must teach them how to be more confident communicating with colleagues who harass, so as to stop the behavior when it occurs and to make an impression on the violator going forward—all in a manner that does not wreck the victim's career. Men and bystanders can make a difference by participating. We hope this book has helped with those efforts.

Aside from learning how to handle and modify the behavior of workplace colleagues who bully, discriminate, and sexually harass, women (and men) must also learn how to add value and how to engender trust and confidence with their superiors, colleagues, and clients, whether male or female. Both JR and I believe we did that successfully. Most of our advice is common sense and practical. Tune in to our next book, *Play Smart*, for our view on how to achieve and make a difference at work, one building block at a time, specifically in a male-dominated environment.

# Acknowledgments

JR and I would like to thank our family and friends for their support and continuous participation in discussions of the subject matter of sexual harassment, and especially our husbands David and Rob, who are undoubtedly exhausted from the constant attention to the topic. From our friends and colleagues who participated in numerous focus group happy hours to discuss personal experiences and responses that either worked or didn't, to our numerous and rewarding lunch, happy hour, and dinner discussions with our favorite male friends Jack Loughrey, Rob Hargis, Willy Geiler, Keith Sepessy, Jeff Blackman, and Brian Hughes—you helped us dissect current events and supplied great feedback on how best to handle inappropriate behavior.

Special thanks to the contributors who made a difference in the initial drafting of this book, including our friends at Bright Social Agency (Cris, Martin, and Angie), Hailey Hobren (a fellow attorney), our editor at Brown Books Publishing, Darla Bruno, and most importantly, Milli Brown, who is a strong supporter of the #MeToo movement and the purpose of this book. We could not have done it without all of you.

Finally, we must thank our parents, who taught us self-respect and encouraged us to be confident and brave. We love you.

# Notes

## Introduction

1. Mia Mercado, "Sexual Harassment at Work Is Far Too Common," *Bustle*, June 15, 2018, https://www.bustle.com/p/how-common-is-sexual-harassment-at-work-almost-1-in-3-women-have-experienced-it-according-to-a-new-poll-54068.

2. "Sexual Harassment," US Equal Employment Opportunity Commission, www.eeoc.gov/laws/types/sexual_harassment.cfm.

3. Kate Germano, "Here's How the Corps Still Needs to Change a Year after Marines United," *Task & Purpose*, March 5, 2018, https://taskandpurpose.com/marines-united-address-problems/.

4. Wikipedia, s.v. "misogyny," accessed July 27 2018, en.wikipedia.org/wiki/Misogyny.

5. Hanna Kozlowska, "There Is Only One Way to Undo Decades of Ingrained Institutional Sexism in the US Military," *Quartz*, March 20, 2017, https://qz.com/935983/recruiting-more-women-is-the-best-way-to-solve-one-of-the-us-militarys-worst-problems/.

6. The North Atlantic Treaty Organization is an alliance or group of countries from Europe and North America formed in 1949 to protect and defend the people and territory of its members. "10 Things You Need to Know about Nato," NATO, https://www.nato.int/cps/su/natohq/126169.htm.

7. Craig Whitlock, "How the Military Handles Sexual Assault Cases behind Closed Doors," *Washington Post*, September 30, 2017, https://www.washingtonpost.com/investigations/how-the-military-handles-sexual-assault-cases-behind-closed-doors/2017/09/30/a9df0682-672a-11e7-a1d7-9a32c91c6f40_story.html?utm_term=.f50cbb72e3e7.

8. Lolita C Baldor, "Pentagon: More Sex Harassment, Retribution Cases in Military," WPXI, April 30, 2018, https://www.wpxi.com/news/pentagon-more-sex-harassment-retribution-cases-in-military/741570194.

9. Antonieta Rico, "Why Military Women Are Missing from the #MeToo Movement," *Time*, December 12, 2017, http://time.com/5060570/military-women-sexual-assault/.

10. Kirsten Gillebrand, US Senator for New York, "With Scandal after Scandal in the Military, Gillibrand Stands with Bipartisan Group of Senators to Demand Congress Finally Address Crisis of Military Sexual Assault and Protect Service Members," news release, November 16, 2017, www.gillibrand.senate.gov/news/press/release/with-scandal-after-scandal-in-the-military-gillibrand-stands-with-bipartisan-group-of-senators-to-demand-congress-finally-address-crisis-of-military-sexual-assault-and-protect-service-members.

11. "Military Justice Improvement Act," Kirsten Hillibrand, US Senator for New York, https://www.gillibrand.senate.gov/mjia.

12. Thomas James Brennan, "Hundreds of Marines Investigated for Sharing Photos of Naked Colleagues," *Reveal,* March 4, 2017, https://www.revealnews.org/blog/hundreds-of-marines-investigated-for-sharing-photos-of-naked-colleagues/.

13. Ray Sanchez, "Marines Create Task Force amid Nude Photos Uproar," CNN, March 10, 2017, https://www.cnn.com/2017/03/10/us/military-nude-photos-uproar-neller/index.html.

14. Kate Germano, "Here's How the Corps Still Needs to Change a Year after Marines United," *Task & Purpose*, March 5, 2018, https://taskandpurpose.com/marines-united-address-problems/.

15. Sandra Pearson, "I Am Not a *'Disgrace to Women'* because I Don't Support the Women's March,"Medium post, January 22, 2017, medium.com/@sandrakpears2014/i-am-not-a-disgrace-to-women-because-i-dont-support-the-women-s-march-731c04835e08.

16. Dina Leygerman, "You Are Not Equal. I'm Sorry," Medium post, January 23, 2017, https://medium.com/@dinachka82/about-your-poem-1f26a7585a6f. Dina Leygerman is a staff writer for Romper and blogger whose work has appeared in *Elle, HuffPost, Women's Health*, and the *Independent.*

17. "United States Ranks 45th in Gender Equality,"*Entity,*March 10,2018,https://www.entitymag.com/united-states-ranks-45th-in-gender-equality/; World Economic Forum, "Rankings," *Global Gender Gap Report 2016*, http://reports.weforum.org/global-gender-gap-report-2016/rankings/?doing_wp_cron=1533846502.076368093 4906005859375.

18. *Merriam-Webster Online,* s.v. "feminism," www.merriam-webster.com/dictionary/feminism.

19. Vocabulary.com, s.v. "feminist," www.vocabulary.com/dictionary/feminist.

20. Suzannah Weiss, "7 Things the Word 'Feminist' Does NOT Mean," *Bustle,* July 5,

2016, https://www.bustle.com/articles/170721-7-things-the-word-feminist-does-not-mean.

# Chapter 1

1. Amber Phillips, "The Wave of Sexual Harassment Allegations Is Finally Hitting Congress," *Washington Post*, November 16, 2017, https://www.washingtonpost.com/news/the-fix/wp/2017/11/16/the-wave-of-sexual-harassment-allegations-is-finally-hitting-congress/?utm_term=.9948c1a5e5d1.

2. Michelle Ye Hee Lee and Elise Viebeck, "How Congress Plays by Different Rules on Sexual Harassment and Misconduct," *Washington Post*, October 27, 2017, https://www.washingtonpost.com/politics/how-congress-plays-by-different-rules-on-sexual-harassment-and-misconduct/2017/10/26/2b9a8412-b80c-11e7-9e58-e6288544af98_story.html?utm_term=.58498665ffc2.

3. Daniella Diaz and Sunlen Serafaty, "House Passes Bill to Address Sexual Harassment in Congress," CNN, February 6, 2018, www.cnn.com/2018/02/06/politics/house-sexual-harassment-bill/index.html.

4. Maya Rhodan, "Senate Women Call for Vote on Sexual Harassment Bill," *Time*, March 28, 2018, time.com/5218765/congress-sexual-harassment-legislation/.

5. Juliet Linderman, "Senate Approves Bill That Would Change How Sexual Harassment Is Handled in Congress," PBS, May 24, 2018, www.pbs.org/newshour/politics/senate-approves-bill-that-would-change-how-sexual-harassment-is-handled-in-congress.

6. Jennifer Bendery, "Civil Rights Groups Rip Senate for Weak Overhaul of Sexual Harassment Policy," *HuffPost*, May 31, 2018, www.huffingtonpost.com/entry/civil-rights-groups-senate-bill-sexual-harassment-policy_us_5b0714e3e4b07c4ea1066816.

7. Associated Press, "State Legislatures Considering Beefing Up Sexual Harassment Policies after Wave of Misconduct Revelations," *Business Insider*, January 11, 2018, www.businessinsider.com/state-legislatures-considering-beefing-up-sexual-harassment-policies-2018-1.

8. "Title VII, Civil Rights Act of 1964, as Amended," United States Department of Labor, accessed July 31, 2018, www.dol.gov/oasam/regs/statutes/2000e-16.htm.

9. Meritor Savings Bank, FSB v. Vinson, 477 U.S. 57 (1986), scholar.google.com/scholar_case?case=14616838878214701501.

10. Burlington Industries, Inc. v. Ellerth, 524 U.S. 742 (1998), scholar.google.com/

scholar_case?case=2707173104214869053; Faragher v. City of Boca Raton, 524 U.S. 775 (1998), Legal Information Institute, www.law.cornell.edu/supct/html/97-282. ZO.html.

11. Prior to these cases, courts and legal commentators differentiated between "quid pro quo" sexual harassment (sex for a raise) and "hostile work environment" sexual harassment (similar to the "severe and pervasive" standard referenced in this chapter).

12. "Supervisor" is defined as a person the employer has empowered "to take tangible employment actions against the victim . . . such as hiring, firing, failing to promote, reassignment with significantly different responsibilities, or a decision causing a significant change in benefits." Vance v. Ball State University, 133 S. Ct. 2434 (2013), scholar.google.com/scholar_case?case=14881304984289805523.

   The Vance case narrowed the previous definition of the EEOC, which included anyone with the ability to exercise "significant direction" over another person's daily work, even if they could not hire, fire, or make other major employment decisions. The court decision essentially eliminated any team or shift leaders from the definition of supervisors, as well as potentially any supervisor who harasses an employee who works outside of his or her department. Jonathan Cohn, "New and Narrower Definition of 'Supervisor,'" Stember Cohn & Davidson-Welling, November 8, 2013, https://stembercohn.com/supreme-court-narrows-definition-of-supervisor-making-harassment-cases-more-challenging-for-employees/.

13. *Ellerth*, 524 U.S. at 753.

14. *Ellerth*, 524 U.S. at 761.

15. *Meritor*, 477 U.S. at 67.

16. *Faragher*, 524 U.S. at 788.

17. Anderson v. G.D.C., Inc., 281 F.3d 452 (4th Cir. 2002), scholar.google.com/scholar_case?case=970530703788685226.

18. Harris v. Forklift Sys., 510 U.S. 17 (1993), Legal Information Institute, www.law.cornell.edu/supct/html/92-1168.ZO.html.

19. Roebuck v. Washington, 408 F.3d 790 (D.C. Cir. 2005), scholar.google.com/scholar_case?case=7683864893603170872.

20. The Ellerth and Faragher cases also established affirmative defenses to employer liability for sexual harassment by a supervisor, consisting of two necessary elements. The first element requires the employer to exercise "reasonable care" to prevent and promptly correct any harassing behavior. Reasonable care might include establishing anti-sexual-harassment policies and procedures for complaint, disseminating such policies to and educating employees, and enforcing such policies and procedures

effectively. The second element requires the employee to have unreasonably failed to take advantage of any preventive or corrective opportunities provided by the employer or to otherwise avoid harm. If the employer can prove that the employee failed to take advantage of the employer's anti-sexual-harassment policies and procedures and that such failure was unreasonable, the employer may be able to avoid liability. *Ellerth*, 118 S. Ct. at 2270; *Faragher*, 118 S. Ct. at 2293.

21. 29 C.F.R. § 1604.11, Legal Information Institute, www.law.cornell.edu/cfr/text/29/1604.11.

22. "Facts about Sexual Harassment," US Equal Employment Opportunity Commission, last modified June 27, 2002, www.eeoc.gov/facts/fs-sex.html.

23. Ibid.

24. In 1998, the court held that same-sex harassment of a man by a man or of a woman by a woman can be actionable under Title VII. Oncale v. Sundowner Offshore Services, Inc., 523 U.S. 75 (1998).

25. "Sexual Harassment," US Equal Employment Opportunity Commission, www.eeoc.gov/laws/types/sexual_harassment.cfm.

26. Jane Mayer and Ronan Farrow, "Four Women Accuse New York's Attorney General of Physical Abuse," *New Yorker,* May 7, 2018, https://www.newyorker.com/news/news-desk/four-women-accuse-new-yorks-attorney-general-of-physical-abuse.

27. NY AG Underwood, Twitter post, April 16, 2018, 1:54 p.m., twitter.com/newyorkstateag/status/985984777596612610?lang=en.

28. Mayer and Farrow, "Four Women Accuse New York's Attorney General."

29. An Phung and Chloe Melas, "Women Accuse Morgan Freeman of Inappropriate Behavior, Harassment," CNN, May 25, 2018, https://www.cnn.com/2018/05/24/entertainment/morgan-freeman-accusations/index.html.

30. Wandera Hussein, "Morgan Freeman Responds to Sexual Harassment Allegations: 'I did not assault women,'" *Fader,* May 26, 2018, http://www.thefader.com/2018/05/26/morgan-freeman-sexual-allegations-statement.

31. Anita Busch, "Morgan Freeman: Visa Pulls Marketing as Sexual Harassment Fallout Continues," *Deadline Hollywood,* May 24, 2018, http://deadline.com/2018/05/morgan-freeman-visa-pulls-marketing-sexual-harassment-fallout-continues-1202397816/.

32. Melena Ryzik et al., "Louis C.K. Is Accused of Sexual Misconduct by 5 Women," *New York Times,* November 9, 2017, https://www.nytimes.com/2017/11/09/arts/television/louis-ck-sexual-misconduct.html?smid=tw-share.

33. "Company Information," Uber Newsroom, https://www.uber.com/newsroom/company-info/; Artyon Dogtiev, "Uber Revenue and Usage Statistics 2017," Business of Apps, January 9, 2018, http://www.businessofapps.com/data/uber-statistics/.

34. Susan Fowler, "Reflecting on One Very, Very Strange Year at Uber," February 19, 2017, https://www.susanjfowler.com/blog/2017/2/19/reflecting-on-one-very-strange-year-at-uber.

35. Yuki Noguchi, "Uber Fires 20 Employees after Internal Investigation into Sexual Harassment," NPR, June 6, 2017, https://www.npr.org/2017/06/06/531794403/uber-fires-20-employees-after-internal-investigation-into-sexual-harassmen.

36. Anita Balakrishnan, "Here Is the Full 13-Page Report of Recommendations for Uber," CNBC, June 13, 2017, https://www.cnbc.com/2017/06/13/eric-holder-uber-report-full-text.html.

37. Katy Steinmetz and Matt Vella, "Uber Fail: Chaos at the world's most valuable venture-backed company is forcing Uber to question its values," *Time*, June 26, 2017, https://sinapress.ir/directory/photo/safavi/1498036699592844852.pdf.

38. Katy Steinmetz and Matt Vella, "Uber Fail: Upheaval at the World's Most Valuable Startup Is a Wake-Up Call for Silicon Valley," *Time*, June 15, 2017, http://time.com/4819557/uber-fail-upheaval-is-wake-up-call/.

39. Marco della Cava, "Uber Has Lost Market Share to Lyft during Crisis," *USA Today*, June 14, 2017, www.usatoday.com/story/tech/news/2017/06/13/uber-market-share-customer-image-hit-string-scandals/102795024/; Eric Newcomer, "Uber, Lifting Financial Veil, Says Sales Growth Outpaces Losses," *Bloomberg Technology*, April 14, 2017, https://www.bloomberg.com/news/articles/2017-04-14/embattled-uber-reports-strong-sales-growth-as-losses-continue.

40. Nitasha Tiku, "Proposed California Law Targets Sexual Harassment in Venture Capital," *Wired*, August 17, 2017, https://www.wired.com/story/proposed-california-law-targets-sexual-harassment-in-venture-capital/.

41. Erin Griffith, "What Has Tech Done to Fix Its Harassment Problem?" *Wired*, January 22, 2018, https://www.wired.com/story/what-has-tech-done-to-fix-its-harassment-problem/.

# Chapter 2

1. Martha J. Langelan, *Back Off! How to Confront and Stop Sexual Harassment and Harassers* (New York: Fireside, 1993), 34.

2. Ibid., 55, 56.

3. Saskia de Melker, "The Case for Starting Sex Education in Kindergarten," PBS, May 27, 2015, www.pbs.org/newshour/health/spring-fever.

4. Laura Diaz-Zuniga, "South Carolina Students Punished for Spelling 'Rape' with Letters Sprayed on Their Chests," CNN, September 19, 2017, www.cnn.com/2017/09/19/us/sc-students-rape-photo-trnd/index.html.

5. Ibid.

6. For examples of such statistics, I suggest reading the following: Robin McDowell et al., "AP Uncovers 17,000 Reports of Sexual Assaults at Schools across US," Boston.com, May 1, 2017, https://www.boston.com/news/national-news/2017/05/01/ap-uncovers-17000-reports-of-sexual-assaults-at-schools-across-us; Mark Keierleber, "The Younger Victims of Sexual Violence in School," *Atlantic*, August 10, 2017, https://www.theatlantic.com/education/archive/2017/08/the-younger-victims-of-sexual-violence-in-school/536418/; Cindy Long, "The Secret of Sexual Assault in Schools," *NEA Today*, December 4, 2017, http://neatoday.org/2017/12/04/sexual-assault-in-schools/.

7. Amelia Pak-Harvey, "Las Vegas High School Student Arrested at Home in Rape Case," *Las Vegas Review-Journal*, January 18, 2018, https://www.reviewjournal.com/crime/sex-crimes/las-vegas-high-school-student-arrested-at-home-in-rape-case/.

8. Diana Lambert, "Hundreds Walk out of McClatchy High to Protest Handling of Gang Rape and Sex Harassment Cases," *Sacramento Bee*, March 21, 2018, http://www.sacbee.com/news/local/education/article206205709.html.

9. Emanuella Grinberg and Samira Said, "Police: At least 40 People Watched Teen's Sexual Assault on Facebook Live," CNN, March 22, 2017, https://www.cnn.com/2017/03/21/us/facebook-live-gang-rape-chicago/index.html.

10. Aamer Madhani, "Second Juvenile, 15, Arrested in Facebook Live Gang Rape," *USA Today*, April 4, 2017, www.usatoday.com/story/news/2017/04/03/second-juvenile-15-arrested-facebook-live-gang-rape/99999198/.

11. "Effects of Sexual Violence," RAINN, www.rainn.org/effects-sexual-violence; Veena Luthra, "The Trauma of Childhood Sexual Abuse," Anxiety.org, October 1, 2014, www.anxiety.org/understanding-trauma-childhood-sexual-abuse; "The Impact of Child Sexual Abuse on Mental Health," *Child Family Community Australia* 11 (January 2013), Australian Institute of Family Studies, aifs.gov.au/cfca/publications/long-term-effects-child-sexual-abuse/impact-child-sexual-abuse-mental-health.

12. Sean Rossman, "A Year Ago, Penn State's Tim Piazza Died, and His Parents Aren't Letting Up," *USA Today*, February 1, 2018, www.usatoday.com/story/news/nation-now/2018/02/01/penn-state-tim-piazza-hazing-drinking-fraternities/1078862001/.

13. "First Guilty Plea in Penn State Frat Hazing Death of Timothy Piazza," NBC News, www.nbcnews.com/storyline/hazing-in-america/first-guilty-plea-penn-state-frat-hazing-death-timothy-piazza-n882951.

14. Title IX of the Education Amendments of 1972, 20 U.S.C. A§ 1681 et. seq., https://www.justice.gov/crt/overview-title-ix-education-amendments-1972-20-usc-1681-et-seq.

15. Nick Anderson, "At First, 55 Schools Faced Sexual Violence Investigations. Now the List Has Quadrupled," *Washington Post*, January 18, 2017, www.washingtonpost.com/news/grade-point/wp/2017/01/18/at-first-55-schools-faced-sexual-violence-investigations-now-the-list-has-quadrupled/?utm_term=.74d4eb197615.

16. Brad Reagan, "Baylor Regents Found Alleged Sexual Assaults by Football Players 'Horrifying,'" *Wall Street Journal*, October 28, 2016, www.wsj.com/articles/baylor-details-horrifying-alleged-sexual-assaults-by-football-players-1477681988.

17. Bruce Tomaso, "A Quick, Complete Guide to the Baylor Football Sex-Assault Scandal," *Dallas Morning News*, June 1, 2016, https://www.dallasnews.com/news/crime/2016/04/14/how-a-sexual-assault-scandal-engulfed-baylors-football-program.

18. Alyssa Milano, Twitter post, October 15, 2017, 1:21 p.m., https://twitter.com/Alyssa_Milano/status/919659438700670976.

19. Note that another, less well known "me too" movement was founded in 2006 by community organizer Tarana Burke to spread awareness about sexual assault in lower-income communities of color. As Ms. Burke explained, "[Me Too] was a catchphrase to be used from survivor to survivor to let folks know that they were not alone and that a movement for radical healing was happening and possible." Zahara Hill, "A Black Woman Created the 'Me Too' Campaign Against Sexual Assault 10 Years Ago," *Ebony*, October 18, 2017, http://www.ebony.com/news-views/black-woman-me-too-movement-tarana-burke-alyssa-milano.

20. Jodi Kantor and Megan Twohey, "Harvey Weinstein Paid Off Sexual Harassment Accusers for Decades," *New York Times*, 5 October 2017, https://www.nytimes.com/2017/10/05/us/harvey-weinstein-harassment-allegations.html.

21. Rebecca Traister, "Why the Harvey Weinstein Sexual-Harassment Allegations Didn't Come Out Until Now," *Cut*, October 5, 2017, https://www.thecut.com/2017/10/why-the-weinstein-sexual-harassment-allegations-came-out-now.html.

22. Erin Gloria Ryan, "When Powerful Men Enable Powerful Predators," *Daily Beast*, October 9, 2017, www.thedailybeast.com/when-powerful-men-enable-powerful-predators.

23. Tim Stelloh, "Ashley Judd Sues Weinstein, Alleging Sexual Harassment, Retaliation," NBC News, April 30, 2018, https://www.nbcnews.com/news/us-news/ashely-judd-sues-harvey-weinstein-sexual-harassment-retaliation-n870286.

24. Elahe Izadi, "The Weinstein Co. Declares Bankruptcy. Here's What That Means and What Could Be Next," *Washington Post*, March 20, 2018, https://www.washingtonpost.com/news/arts-and-entertainment/wp/2018/03/20/the-weinstein-company-declares-bankruptcy-heres-what-that-means-and-what-could-be-next/?utm_term=.d6f0bf0c0d46.

25. Reuters, "Film Producer Weinstein Indicted for Rape: New York Prosecutor," May 30, 2018, www.reuters.com/article/us-people-harvey-weinstein/film-producer-weinstein-indicted-for-rape-new-york-prosecutor-idUSKCN1IV2UT?wpmm=1.

26. Ibid.

27. James C. Mckinley et al., "Harvey Weinstein Will Be Arrested and Charged With Rape, Officials Say," *New York Times*, May 24, 2018, www.nytimes.com/2018/05/24/nyregion/harvey-weinstein-arrest-new-york.html?emc=edit_nn_20180525.

28. Glenn Whipp, "38 Women Have Come forward to Accuse Director James Toback of Sexual Harassment," *Los Angeles Times*, October 22, 2017, http://beta.latimes.com/entertainment/la-et-mn-james-toback-sexual-harassment-allegations-20171018-story.html.

29. Jane Mayer, "Anita Hill on Weinstein, Trump, and a Watershed Moment for Sexual Harassment Accusations," *New Yorker*, April 23, 2018, https://www.newyorker.com/news/news-desk/anita-hill-on-weinstein-trump-and-a-watershed-moment-for-sexual-harassment-accusations?mbid=nl_Daily%20110217.

30. Ronan Farrow, "Weighing the Costs of Speaking Out about Harvey Weinstein," *New Yorker*, October 27, 2017, https://www.newyorker.com/news/news-desk/weighing-the-costs-of-speaking-out-about-harvey-weinstein.

31. Chloe Melas, "'House of Cards' Employees Allege Sexual Harassment, Assault by Kevin Spacey," CNNMoney, November 3, 2017, http://money.cnn.com/2017/11/02/media/house-of-cards-kevin-spacey-harassment/index.html.

32. David Robb, "Producers Guild Sets Anti-Sexual Harassment Guidelines," *Deadline Hollywood*, January 19, 2018, http://deadline.com/2018/01/sexual-harassment-guidelines-producers-guild-1202248420/.

33. Foundation Center, "$15 Million Legal Defense Fund to Fight Sexual Harassment Announced," *Philanthropy News Digest*, January 3, 2018, philanthropynewsdigest. org/news/15-million-legal-defense-fund-to-fight-sexual-harassment-announced.

34. Claire Cain Miller, "David Schwimmer Made Six Short Films About Sexual Harassment. We Annotate One of Them," *New York Times*, January 26, 2018, www. nytimes.com/interactive/2018/01/26/upshot/sexual-harassment-script-react.html.

# Chapter 3

1. Martha J. Langelan, *Back Off! How to Confront and Stop Sexual Harassment and Harassers* (New York: Fireside, 1993), 42–50.

2. Ibid., 44.

3. Ibid., 49.

4. Ibid., 46.

5. Maya Kosoff, "Mass Firings at Uber as Sexual Harassment Scandal Grows," Hive, *Vanity Fair*, June 6, 2017, www.vanityfair.com/news/2017/06/uber-fires-20-employees-harassment-investigation.

6. Leaving the door open will allow you to better control his reaction to your confrontation. It is better to bring a witness if possible.

7. In defining "basis," for example, the EEOC will look "at the whole record: the circumstances, such as the nature of the sexual advances, and the context in which the alleged incidents occurred. A determination on the allegations is made from the facts on a case-by-case basis." "Facts About Sexual Harassment," US Equal Employment Opportunity Commission, last modified June 27, 2002, www.eeoc.gov/facts/fs-sex. html.

8. "Damages" can include *compensatory damages* (loss of employment ability and wages, for example, or medical expenses), *emotional damages* (such as intentional infliction of emotional distress), and *punitive damages*, including attorney's fees (when the harasser's misconduct is particularly egregious, outrageous, malicious, or otherwise shocks the conscious of the jury). There are limits on the amount of compensatory and punitive damages a person can recover, and the limits vary on the size of the employer. "Remedies For Employment Discrimination," US Equal Employment Opportunity Commission, www.eeoc.gov/employees/remedies.cfm.

9. "Time Limits for Filing a Charge," US Equal Employment Opportunity Commission, www.eeoc.gov/employees/timeliness.cfm.

10. "Filing a Lawsuit," US Equal Employment Opportunity Commission, www.eeoc. gov/employees/lawsuit.cfm.

11. Ibid.

12. Emily Steel and Michael S. Schmidt, "Bill O'Reilly Thrives at Fox News, Even as Harassment Settlements Add Up," *New York Times*, April 1, 2017, www.nytimes. com/2017/04/01/business/media/bill-oreilly-sexual-harassment-fox-news.html; Maya Kosoff, "Mass Firings at Uber as Sexual Harassment Scandal Grows," Hive, *Vanity Fair*, June 6, 2017, www.vanityfair.com/news/2017/06/uber-fires-20-employees-harassment-investigation.

13. Margaret Sullivan, "'I Felt Angry That It Took so Long': Gretchen Carlson on Roger Ailes's Ouster from Fox News," *Washington Post*, July 28, 2016, www. washingtonpost.com/lifestyle/style/i-felt-angry-that-it-took-so-long-gretchen-carlson-on-roger-ailess-ouster-from-fox-news/2016/07/28/33a065f6-54c0-11e6-b7de-dfe509430c39_story.html?utm_term=.7638cb59e150.

14. Manuel Roig-Franzia, Scott Higham, Paul Farhi, and Krissah Thompson, "The Fall of Roger Ailes: He Made Fox News His 'Locker Room' – and Now Women Are Telling Their Stories," *Washington Post*, July 22, 2016, https://www.washingtonpost. com/lifestyle/style/the-fall-of-roger-ailes-he-made-fox-his-locker-room--and-now-women-are-telling-their-stories/2016/07/22/5eff9024-5014-11e6-aa14-e0c1087f7583_story.html?tid=a_inl&utm_term=.a6a57a02bc91.

15. Michael M. Grynbaum and John Koblin, "Fox Settles with Gretchen Carlson over Roger Ailes Sex Harassment Claims," *New York Times*, September 6, 2016, https:// www.nytimes.com/2016/09/07/business/media/fox-news-roger-ailes-gretchen-carlson-sexual-harassment-lawsuit-settlement.html.

16. Joe Flint, "Roger Ailes Steps Down from Fox News with $40 Million Exit Package," MarketWatch, July 21, 2016, www.marketwatch.com/story/roger-ailes-steps-down-from-fox-news-with-40-million-exit-package-2016-07-21.

17. Emily Steel and Michael S. Schmidt, "Fox News Settled Sexual Harassment Allegations against Bill O'Reilly, Documents Show," *New York Times*, January 10, 2017, www.nytimes.com/2017/01/10/business/media/bill-oreilly-sexual-harassment-fox-news-juliet-huddy.html.

18. Emily Steel and Michael S. Schmidt, "Bill O'Reilly Settled New Harassment Claim, Then Fox Renewed His Contract," *New York Times*, October 21, 2017, https:// www.nytimes.com/2017/10/21/business/media/bill-oreilly-sexual-harassment. html.

19.  Maxwell Tani, "'Don't Be Sarcastic': Matt Lauer Confronts Bill O'Reilly about Sexual-Harassment Claims in Tense Interview," *Business Insider,* September 19, 2017, http://www.businessinsider.com/matt-lauer-bill-oreilly-interview-sexual-harassment-2017-9.

20.  "I'm not interested in making my network look bad. At all. That doesn't interest me one bit," O'Reilly said on CBS. "Bill O'Reilly Suggests Megyn Kelly Is Making Fox News Look Bad," CNNMoney, money.cnn.com/2016/11/15/media/megyn-kelly-bill-oreilly-book/index.html.

21.  Graham Lanktree, "21st Century Fox Payouts over Fox News Sexual Harassment Claims Rise to $85 million," *Newsweek,* April 21, 2017, http://www.newsweek.com/fox-news-payouts-rise-85-million-over-sexual-harassment-claims-587361.

22.  Gabriel Sherman, "Women Can Wear Pants on Fox News Now, but Not Much Else Has Changed," *New York Magazine,* May 14, 2017, http://nymag.com/daily/intelligencer/2017/05/rupert-murdoch-disaster-at-fox-news.html.

23.  Paul Farhi, "A New CEO at Fox News, Suzanne Scott, Comes with Baggage from the Ailes Years," *Washington Post,* May 17, 2018, https://www.washingtonpost.com/lifestyle/style/a-new-ceo-at-fox-news-suzanne-scott-comes-with-baggage-from-the-ailes-years/2018/05/17/d30f6cc8-59ef-11e8-858f-12becb4d6067_story.html?utm_term=.2500e36baa27.

24.  Mandatory arbitration is a form of alternative dispute resolution in which two or more parties are required to submit their dispute to a third party arbitrator, as opposed to filing a legal action in a court of law. If agreement has been reached by the parties, the resolution is binding. Dictionary.com defines "binding arbitration" as "a judgment made by a third party to settle a dispute between two other parties, which is obligatory (both parties agree in advance to abide by the result." Dictionary.com, s.v. "binding arbitration," accessed May 5, 2018, http://www.dictionary.com/browse/binding-arbitration.

25.  Emily Steel and Michael S. Schmidt, "Bill O'Reilly Thrives at Fox News, Even as Harassment Settlements Add Up," *New York Times,* April 1, 2017, www.nytimes.com/2017/04/01/business/media/bill-oreilly-sexual-harassment-fox-news.html.

26.  "Time's Up Now," Time's Up, https://www.timesupnow.com.

27.  Maya Kosoff, "Mass Firings at Uber as Sexual Harassment Scandal Grows," Hive, *Vanity Fair,* June 6, 2017, www.vanityfair.com/news/2017/06/uber-fires-20-employees-harassment-investigation.

# Chapter 4

1. Todd VanDerWerff, "Assholes, Job Dependency, and Intimacy: 3 Reasons It's Hard to End Harassment in Hollywood," *Vox*, November 17, 2017, https://www.vox.com/culture/2017/11/17/16651316/hollywood-harassment-why.

2. Sandrea Newman, "What Kind of Person Makes False Rape Accusations," *Quartz*, May 11, 2017, https://qz.com/980766/the-truth-about-false-rape-accusations/; Lisa Lazard, "Here's the Truth about False Accusations of Sexual Violence," Conversation, November 24, 2017, https://theconversation.com/heres-the-truth-about-false-accusations-of-sexual-violence-88049.

# Chapter 6

1. Jon Wertheim and Michael McCann, "Exclusive: Inside the Mavericks' Corrosive Workplace," *Sports Illustrated*, www.si.com/nba/2018/02/20/dallas-mavericks-sexual-misconduct-investigation-mark-cuban-response?utm_campaign=sinow.

2. Adam Jezard, "Why We Need to Calculate the Economic Costs of Sexual Harassment," *Global Agenda* (blog), World Economic Forum, October 23, 2017, https://www.weforum.org/agenda/2017/10/why-we-need-to-calculate-the-economic-costs-of-sexual-harassment/.

3. Lynn Parramore, "$MeToo: The Economic Cost of Sexual Harassment," Institute for New Economic Thinking, January 2018, https://www.ineteconomics.org/research/research-papers/metoo-the-economic-cost-of-sexual-harassment.

4. "Charges Alleging Sex-Based Harassment (Charges Filed with EEOC) FY 2010 - FY 2017," Equal Employment Opportunity Commission, www.eeoc.gov/eeoc/statistics/enforcement/sexual_harassment_new.cfm.

5. Jafa-Bodden v. Choudhury, No. BC512041 (Los Angeles Sup. Ct. Feb. 22, 2016); as modified, (Los Angeles Sup. Ct. April 13, 2016), reducing punitive damages award to $4.6 million.

6. Nathan Bomey, "Sexual Harassment Went Unchecked for Decades as Payouts Silenced Accusers," *USA Today*, December 2, 2017, www.usatoday.com/story/money/business/2017/12/01/sexual-harassment-went-unchecked-decades-payouts-silenced-accusers/881070001/.

7. Aditya Shrivastava, "5 Companies That Went Down because of Sexual Harassment Complaints and What Others Need to Learn from Them," YourStory, February 10,

2018, https://yourstory.com/2018/02/5-companies-sexual-harassment-complaints/.

8. Peter Blumberg, "Uber Wants Pay Inequality Accord to Also Settle Sex Harassment Claims," *Insurance Journal,* April 10, 2018, https://www.insurancejournal.com/news/national/2018/04/10/485867.htm.

9. Emily Shugerman, "Sexual Harassment Costs Fox News up to $110 million in Last Nine Months," *Independent,* May 11, 2017, http://www.independent.co.uk/news/world/americas/fox-news-sexual-harassment-cases-payouts-settlements-bill-o-reilly-roger-ailes-a7730556.html.

10. Brent Lang and Justin Kroll, "Replacing Kevin Spacey on 'All the Money in the World' Will Cost Millions," *Variety,* November 10, 2017, http://variety.com/2017/film/news/kevin-spacey-christopher-plummer-all-the-money-in-the-world-1202611975/.

11. Ronan Farrow, "Les Moonves and CBS Face Allegations of Sexual Misconduct," *New Yorker,* July 28, 2018, https://www.newyorker.com/magazine/2018/08/06/les-moonves-and-cbs-face-allegations-of-sexual-misconduct?mbid=nl_Daily%20 072818; Todd Spangler, "CBS Stock Tumbles on Reports of Sexual-Harassment Allegations Against CEO Leslie Moonves," *Variety,* July 27, 2018, https://variety.com/2018/biz/news/cbs-stock-tumbles-on-sexual-harassment-allegations-against-ceo-leslie-moonves-1202888222/.

12. theBoardlist, "5 Reasons Why Having Women in Leadership Benefits Your Entire Company," Medium post, September 5, 2016, https://mediuKm.com/@ theBoardlist/5-reasons-why-having-women-in-leadership-benefits-your-entire-company-labor-day-2016-a3e46162a7a0; Marcus Noland and Tyler Moran, "Study: Firms with More Women in the C-Suite Are More Profitable," *Harvard Business Review,* February 8, 2016, https://hbr.org/2016/02/study-firms-with-more-women-in-the-c-suite-are-more-profitable.

13. Catalyst Information Center, *Why Diversity Matters,* July 2013, http://www.catalyst.org/system/files/why_diversity_matters_catalyst_0.pdf.

14. Georges Desvaux and Sandrine Devillard, "Women Matter 2: Female leadership, a Competitive Edge for the Future," McKinsey & Company, May 6, 2018, https://www.mckinsey.com/~/media/McKinsey/Business%20Functions/Organization/Our%20 Insights/Women%20matter/Women_matter_oct2008_english.ashx.

15. Sangeeta Bharadwaj Badal, "The Business Benefits of Gender Diversity," *Gallup Business Journal,* January 20, 2014, http://news.gallup.com/businessjournal/166220/business-benefits-gender-diversity.aspx.

16. David Rock and Heidi Grant, "Why Diverse Teams Are Smarter," *Harvard*

*Business Review*, November 4, 2016, https://hbr.org/2016/11/why-diverse-teams-are-smarter.

17. Katie Shonk, "Challenges Facing Women Negotiators: The Impact of Leadership Styles on Strategic Decisions," *Program on Negotiation* (blog), Harvard Law School, February 18, 2018, https://www.pon.harvard.edu/daily/leadership-skills-daily/women-and-negotiation-leveling-the-playing-field/.

18. Lisa Gates, "Why Women Are Better Negotiators Than Men," *Forbes*, August 5, 2011, https://www.forbes.com/sites/shenegotiates/2011/08/05/why-women-are-better-negotiators-than-men/#1789e0d57f72.

19. John Detrixhe, "CEOs of Big UK Companies Are Reluctant to Commit to Promoting Women to Top Roles," *Quartz at Work*, January 9, 2018, https://work.qz.com/1175275/30-club-only-14-of-the-uks-ftse-100-companies-have-committed-to-promoting-women-to-30-of-top-roles/.

20. Implicit bias refers to when we have attitudes toward people or associate stereotypes with them without our conscious knowledge—preconceived, improper notions of gender and normative gender behavior. Wendi S. Lazar, Terese M. Connolly, and Gregory Chiarello, *Zero Tolerance; Best Practices for Combating Sex-Based Harassment in the Legal Profession* (American Bar Association, 2018); "Implicit Bias Explained," Perception Institute, https://perception.org/research/implicit-bias/.

21. Lucy Shea, "Why Aren't There More Women in Leadership Positions?" GenFKD, October 23, 2017, http://www.genfkd.org/arent-women-leadership-positions.

22. Alanna Petroff, "Germany's New 30% Rule for Women on Boards," CNNMoney, March 8, 2015, http://money.cnn.com/2015/03/06/news/women-boards-germany-30/index.html.

23. Renuka Rayasam, "Why Germany's New Quota for Women on Boards Looks Like a Bust," *Fortune,* March 11, 2016, http://fortune.com/2016/03/11/germany-board-quota-women/.

24. Claire Cain Miller, "Unintended Consequences of Sexual Harassment Scandals," Upshot, *New York Times*, October 9, 2017, https://www.nytimes.com/2017/10/09/upshot/as-sexual-harassment-scandals-spook-men-it-can-backfire-for-women.html; John Simmons, "Men Learn How to Be 'Allies,' Without Fear, to Female Colleagues," *Wall Street Journal*, April 4, 2018, https://www.wsj.com/articles/men-learn-how-to-be-allies-without-fear-to-female-colleagues-1522849814.

25. Sara Randazzo and Nicole Hong, "At Law Firms, Rainmakers Accused of Harassment Can Switch Jobs With Ease," *Wall Street Journal,* June 30, 2018, https://www.wsj.

com/articles/at-law-firms-rainmakers-accused-of-harassment-can-switch-jobs-with-ease-1532965126?ns=prod/accounts-wsj&ns=prod/accounts-wsj.

26. Ibid.

27. Davia Temin, "A 15-Point Plan for Boards and CEOs to Eradicate Sexual Harassment in Their Organizations," *Forbes*, January 17, 2018, https://www.forbes.com/sites/daviatemin/2018/01/17/a-15-point-plan-for-boards-and-ceos-to-eradicate-sexual-harassment-in-their-organizations/#3026138f2928.

# Chapter 7

1. The letter was read aloud by Tweeden on an episode of *The View* on November 17, 2017. Max Greenwood, "Franken Sent a Letter to Woman Who Accused Him of Groping," *Hill*, November 17, 2017, http://thehill.com/homenews/senate/360996-franken-sent-a-letter-to-woman-who-accused-him-of-groping.

2. "Franken Will Face Ethics Probe," *Dallas Morning News*, PressReader, November 17, 2017, http://www.pressreader.com/usa/the-dallas-morning-news/20171117/281505046513644.

3. Samantha Cooney, "All the Women Who Have Accused Sen. Al Franken of Sexual Misconduct," *Time*, December 6, 2017, http://time.com/5042931/al-franken-accusers/.

4. "Across America with Carol Costello," CNN, https://www.cnn.com/shows/across-america-carol-costello.

5. Martha J. Langelan, *Back Off! How to Confront and Stop Sexual Harassment and Harassers* (New York: Fireside, 1993), 34.

6. Ibid., 54–58.

7. "Title VII, Civil Rights Act of 1964, as Amended," United States Department of Labor, accessed July 31, 2018, https://www.dol.gov/oasam/regs/statutes/2000e-16.htm.

8. Sasha Cohen, "A Brief History of Sexual Harassment in America before Anita Hill," *Time*, April 11, 2016, http://time.com/4286575/sexual-harassment-before-anita-hill/.

9. Emily Crockett, "The History of Sexual Harassment Explains Why Many Women Wait So Long to Come Forward," *Vox*, July 14, 2016, https://www.vox.com/2016/7/14/12178412/roger-ailes-sexual-harassment-history-women-wait.

10. Nina Renata Aron, "Groping in the Ivy League Led to the First Sexual Harassment

Suit—and Nothing Happened to the Man," *Timeline*, October 20, 2017, https://timeline.com/carmita-wood-sexual-harrassment-f2c537a0e1e8.

11. Enid Nemy, "Women Begin to Speak Out against Sexual Harassment at Work," *New York Times*, August 19, 1975, https://timesmachine.nytimes.com/timesmachine/1975/08/19/76591747.html?pageNumber=38.

12. Kaitlin Menza, "You Have to See *Redbook's* Shocking 1976 Sexual Harassment Survey," *Redbook*, 28 November 2016, https://www.redbookmag.com/life/a47313/1976-sexual-harassment-survey/; Christina L. Smith, "Sexual Harassment of Working Women," University of Nebraska Omaha, May 1, 1983, Page 4, https://digitalcommons.unomaha.edu/cgi/viewcontent.cgi?article=1937&context=studentwork. In the *Redbook* survey, note that the respondents were limited to *Redbook* readers and that approximately nine thousand readers responded to the survey.

13. "Asking for It," *Time*, May 4, 1981, http://content.time.com/time/subscriber/article/0,33009,954748,00.html

14. Ibid.

15. Wesley G. Pippert, "Schlafly: Sexual harassment No Problem for Virtuous Women," United Press International, April 21, 1981, https://www.upi.com/Archives/1981/04/21/Schlafly-Sexual-harassment-no-problem-for-virtuous-women/9257356677200/.

16. "Title VII, Civil Rights Act of 1964, as Amended," United States Department of Labor, accessed July 31, 2018, https://www.dol.gov/oasam/regs/statutes/2000e-16.htm.

17. Barnes v. M. Costle, 561 F.2d 983 (D.C. Cir. 1977), https://openjurist.org/561/f2d/983/barnes-v-m-costle; Williams v. Saxbe, 413 F. Supp. 654 (D.D.C. 1976), https://scholar.google.com/scholar_case?case=4509276829118316000.

18. *Meritor*, 477 U.S. 57.

19. Julia Carpenter, "How Anita Hill Forever Changed the Way We Talk about Sexual Harassment," CNNMoney, November 9, 2017, http://money.cnn.com/2017/10/30/pf/anita-hill-sexual-harassment/index.html.

20. Douglas Robson, "Huge Surge of Sexual-Harassment Cases Hits the Courts," *San Francisco Business Times*, May 18, 1997, https://www.bizjournals.com/sanfrancisco/stories/1997/05/19/focus6.html.

21. "The Year of the Woman, 1992," History, Art, & Archives, US House of Representatives, accessed July 31, 2018, http://history.house.gov/Exhibitions-and-

Publications/WIC/Historical-Essays/Assembling-Amplifying-Ascending/Women-Decade/.

22. "President Clinton Impeached," History.com, accessed July 31, 2018, http://www.history.com/this-day-in-history/president-clinton-impeached.

23. Ibid.

24. Norman Kempster, "What Really Happened at Tailhook Convention: Scandal: The Pentagon Report Graphically Describes How Fraternity-Style Hi-Jinks Turned into Hall of Horrors," *Los Angeles Times*, April 24, 1993, http://articles.latimes.com/1993-04-24/news/mn-26672_1_tailhook-convention.

25. Eric Schmitt, "Wall of Silence Impedes Inquiry into a Rowdy Navy Convention," *New York Times*, June 14, 1992, https://www.nytimes.com/1992/06/14/us/wall-of-silence-impedes-inquiry-into-a-rowdy-navy-convention.html?pagewanted=all&src=pm.

26. Michael Winerip, "Revisiting the Military's Tailhook Scandal," *New York Times*, May 13, 2013, https://www.nytimes.com/2013/05/13/booming/revisiting-the-militarys-tailhook-scandal-video.html; "Legacy of the Tailhook Scandal | Retro Report | The New York Times," YouTube video, 12:41, posted by "The New York Times," May 21, 2013, accessed July 31, 2018, https://www.youtube.com/watch?v=93vW5QZilAw.

27. "Legacy of the Tailhook Scandal | Retro Report | The New York Times," YouTube video, 12:41, posted by "The New York Times," May 21, 2013, accessed July 31, 2018, https://www.youtube.com/watch?v=93vW5QZilAw.

28. "Hilton Ordered to Pay Tailhook Whistle-Blower $1.7 Million," *Washington Post*, October 29, 1994, accessed July 31, 2018, https://www.washingtonpost.com/archive/politics/1994/10/29/hilton-ordered-to-pay-tailhook-whistle-blower-17-million/50b9f6c9-9c29-48fe-806e-52f5678103e8/?utm_term=.cf194775c08b.

29. "Title VII, Civil Rights Act of 1964, as Amended," United States Department of Labor, accessed July 31, 2018, https://www.dol.gov/oasam/regs/statutes/2000e-16.htm.

30. "Legacy of the Tailhook Scandal | Retro Report | The New York Times," YouTube video, 12:41, posted by "The New York Times," May 21, 2013, accessed July 31, 2018, https://www.youtube.com/watch?v=93vW5QZilAw.

31. Lisa N. Sacco, *The Violence Against Women Act: Overview, Legislation, and Federal Funding*, Congressional Research Service, May 26, 2015, https://fas.org/sgp/crs/misc/R42499.pdf; Violence Against Women Act of 1994, Title IV, § 40001–40703 of the Violent Crime Control and Law Enforcement Act, H.R. 3355, Publ. L. No.103–322 (1994), codified in part at 42 U.S.C. § 13701–14040.

32. Matthew K. Fenton, "History of Sexual Harassment Laws in the United States," *Wenzel Fenton Cabassa* (blog), December 28, 2017, accessed July 31, 2018, https://www.wenzelfenton.com/blog/2018/01/01/history-sexual-harassment-laws-united-states/.

33. Stephen Braun, "Mitsubishi to Pay $34 Million in Sex Harassment Case," *Los Angeles Times*, June 12, 1998, http://articles.latimes.com/1998/jun/12/news/mn-59249.

34. Title IX of the Education Amendments of 1972, 20 U.S.C. A§ 1681 et. seq. https://www.justice.gov/crt/overview-title-ix-education-amendments-1972-20-usc-1681-et-seq.

35. Allison Sherry, "CU Settles Case Stemming from Recruit Scandal," *Denver Post*, May 8, 2016, accessed July 31, 2018, https://www.denverpost.com/2007/12/05/cu-settles-case-stemming-from-recruit-scandal/.

36. "Settlement in Sexual Assault Case," Inside Higher Ed's News, December 6, 2007, accessed July 31, 2018, https://www.insidehighered.com/news/2007/12/06/settlement-sexual-assault-case.

37. Kaitlin Menza, "57 Things I Need You to Stop Doing to the Women You Work With," *Esquire*, October 16, 2017, http://www.esquire.com/lifestyle/money/a12845576/what-sexual-harassment-looks-like-examples/.

38. Mary Schmich, "The One-Sentence Guide on Sexual Harassment," *Chicago Tribune*, October 26, 2017, http://www.chicagotribune.com/news/columnists/schmich/ct-met-sexual-harassment-mary-schmich-20171026-story.html.

39. Katie Way, "I Went on a Date with Aziz Ansari. It Turned in to the Worst Night of My Life," *Babe*, January 13, 2018, https://babe.net/2018/01/13/aziz-ansari-28355.

40. "The UK Explained Sexual Consent in the Most British Way Possible," Facebook video, 3:01, from RockStarDinosaurPiratePrincess and Blue Seat Studios, posted by "Insider," November 6, 2015, https://www.facebook.com/thisisinsider/videos/1486796681627725/?hc_ref=ARQX3JiOpBJzQY2BGOh9fHZuiwdaHGCmH3TKbqqQUUj9qnR1H_Y4gLJOSqnqyhyImxM.

41. For more information, visit the following US Equal Employment Opportunity Commission pages: "Title VII of the Civil Rights Act of 1964," https://www.eeoc.gov/laws/statutes/titlevii.cfm; "The Pregnancy Discrimination Act of 1978," https://www.eeoc.gov/laws/statutes/pregnancy.cfm.

42. Barbara Bean-Mellinger, "Male vs Female Statistics in the Workplace in America," *Houston Chronicle*, March 15, 2018, http://work.chron.com/male-vs-female-statistics-workplace-america-23880.html.

43. McKinsey & Company and LeanIn.org, "Getting to gender equality starts with realizing how far we have to go," news release, https://www.prnewswire.com/news-releases/getting-to-gender-equality-starts-with-realizing-how-far-we-have-to-go-300533550.html.

44. Elise Gould and Jessica Schieder, "Black and Hispanic Women Are Paid Substantially Less Than White Men," Economic Policy Institute, March 7, 2017, https://www.epi.org/publication/black-and-hispanic-women-are-hit-particularly-hard-by-the-gender-wage-gap/.

45. Elise Solé, "Why Do People Blame Sexual Harassment on Women's Outfits?" *HuffPost*, December 21, 2017, accessed July 31, 2018, https://www.huffingtonpost.com/entry/why-do-people-blame-sexual-harassment-on-womens-outfits_us_5a3bdbeee4b0b0e5a7a06154.

46. Jessica Wolfendale, "Provocative Dress and Sexual Responsibility," *Georgetown Journal of Gender and the Law* 17, no. 599 (2005): 600, https://philarchive.org/archive/WOLPDA-3.

47. Ibid., 620.

48. Lois Frankel, "Do Women Ever Invite Sexual Harassment?" *Forbes*, October 8, 2010, https://www.forbes.com/sites/work-in-progress/2010/10/08/do-women-ever-invite-sexual-harassment/#3b6998ab49d3.

49. Mana Nakagawa, "Male 'identity threat' can disadvantage women in high status professions," Clayman Institute for Gender Research, Stanford University, April 10, 2014, http://gender.stanford.edu/news/2014/male-identity-threat-can-disadvantage-women-high-status-professions.

50. Julie Creswell, Kevin Draper, and Rachel Abrams, "At Nike, Revolt Led by Women Leads to Exodus of Male Executives," *New York Times*, April 28, 2018, accessed July 31, 2018, https://www.nytimes.com/2018/04/28/business/nike-women.html.

51. Eileen Dooley, "Sexual Harassment Occurs with Women in Power, Too," *Globe and Mail*, March 9, 2018, https://www.theglobeandmail.com/report-on-business/careers/management/sexual-harassment-occurs-with-women-in-power-too/article38245807/.

52. Yashar Ali, "Exclusive: Kimberly Guilfoyle Left Fox News after Investigation into Misconduct Allegations, Sources Say," *HuffPost*, July 27, 2018, accessed July 31, 2018, https://www.huffingtonpost.com/entry/kimberly-guilfoyle-misconduct-allegations-fox-news_us_5b5a6064e4b0b15aba96f4de.

# Chapter 8

1.  Brian Flood, "White House Press Secretary Sarah Sanders Body-Shamed by LA Times Columnist," Fox News, November 4, 2017, http://www.foxnews.com/politics/2017/11/04/white-house-press-secretary-sarah-sanders-body-shamed-by-la-times-columnist.html.

2.  A. J. Katz, "Megyn Kelly Defends Former Fox News Colleagues after Columnist Calls Them as 'Blonde Barbie Dolls,'" *Adweek*, November 8, 2017, accessed July 31, 2018, http://www.adweek.com/tvnewser/megyn-kelly-defends-former-fox-news-colleagues-after-columnist-calls-them-blonde-barbie-dolls/347785.

3.  Steven Zeitchik and Emily Heil, "After Star's Racist Tweet, ABC Pulls the Plug on 'Roseanne,'" *Washington Post*, May 29, 2018, https://www.washingtonpost.com/business/economy/after-stars-racist-tweet-abc-pulls-the-plug-on-roseanne/2018/05/29/5b0d55e8-637a-11e8-a69c-b944de66d9e7_story.html?utm_term=.3f2af449505a.

4.  Kathleen Joyce, "Samantha Bee Apologizes for Vile, 'C-Word' Attack on Ivanka Trump," Fox News, May 31, 2018, http://www.foxnews.com/entertainment/2018/05/31/samantha-bee-calls-ivanka-trump-feckless-c-and-says-should-put-on-something-tight-and-low-cut.html.

5.  "Full Tape with Lewd Donald Trump Remarks (Access Hollywood)," YouTube video, 5:21, from the website of *Access Hollywood*, posted by "Adrian Grummt," October 21, 2016, accessed July 31, 2018, https://www.youtube.com/watch?v=NcZcTnykYbw.

6.  Meghan Keneally, "What Trump Previously Said about the 2005 'Access Hollywood' Tape That He's Now Questioning," ABC News, November 27, 2017, http://abcnews.go.com/US/trump-previously-2005-access-hollywood-tape-now-questioning/story?id=51406745; Samantha Cooney, "These Are the Women Who Have Accused President Trump of Sexual Misconduct," *Time*, December 13, 2017, http://time.com/5058646/donald-trump-accusers/.

7.  Christopher Mele, "Newt Gingrich and Megyn Kelly Get into Bizarre Exchange on Live TV," *New York Times*, October 26, 2016, https://www.nytimes.com/2016/10/26/us/newt-gingrich-megyn-kelly-bizarre-exchange-on-live-tv.html.

8.  "Sexual Assault," United States Department of Justice, accessed July 31, 2018, https://www.justice.gov/ovw/sexual-assault. Emphasis ours.

9.  *Collins English Dictionary Online*, s.v. "boys will be boys," accessed July 31, 2018, https://www.collinsdictionary.com/us/dictionary/english/boys-will-be-boys.

10. Claire Cohen, "Donald Trump Sexism Tracker: Every Offensive Comment in One

Place," *Telegraph,* July 14, 2017, http://www.telegraph.co.uk/women/politics/donald-trump-sexism-tracker-every-offensive-comment-in-one-place/.

11.  Samantha Cooney, "These Are the Women Who Have Accused President Trump of Sexual Misconduct," *Time,* December 13, 2017, http://time.com/5058646/donald-trump-accusers/.

12.  Kindree Cushing, "10 Scandalous Presidential Affairs We've Totally Forgotten About," Listverse, February 24, 2015, https://listverse.com/2015/02/24/10-scandalous-presidential-affairs-weve-totally-forgotten-about/.

13.  Eliza Relman, "Bill Clinton Lashes Out at NBC Interviewer Who Was Grilling Him on the Monica Lewinsky Scandal," *Business Insider,* June 4, 2018, https://www.businessinsider.com/bill-clinton-never-personally-apologized-to-monica-lewinsky-2018-6. Clinton was on a book tour to promote a new thriller he cowrote with author James Patterson, who at one point during the interview defended Clinton: "It's 20 years ago, come on. Let's talk about JFK. Let's talk about, you know, LBJ. Stop already." Amie Parnes, "Bill Clinton Takes Heat for Lack of Apology to Monica Lewinsky," *Hill,* June 5, 2018, http://thehill.com/blogs/blog-briefing-room/390672-bill-clinton-takes-heat-for-lack-of-apology-to-monica-lewinsky.

14.  Richard Shotwell, "NBC News Fires Billy Bush after Lewd Donald Trump Tape Airs," *Chicago Tribune,* October 17, 2016, http://www.chicagotribune.com/entertainment/ct-billy-bush-fired-20161017-story.html.

15.  "Dr. Wendy Walsh Accuses Fox's Bill O'Reilly of Sexual Harassment," *Democracy Now!,* April 4, 2017, accessed July 31, 2018, https://www.democracynow.org/2017/4/4/headlines/dr_wendy_walsh_accuses_foxs_bill_oreilly_of_sexual_harassment.

16.  Audrey Nelson, "Women and the Good Ole Boys Club," *Psychology Today,* March 28, 2017, https://www.psychologytoday.com/us/blog/he-speaks-she-speaks/201703/women-and-the-good-ole-boys-club.

17.  Regina Barreca, *They Used to Call Me Snow White . . . but I Drifted* (New York: Penguin Books, 1990), 125.

# Chapter 9

1.  Paul Samakow, "Forced Arbitration: State Attorneys General Take Sensational Step to End It," *Communities Digital News,* February 18, 2018, https://www.commdiginews.com/business-2/step-ending-forced-arbitration-99172/.

2. Daniela Altimari, "Advocates Press for End to Statute of Limitations for Sexual Assault Crimes," *Hartford Courant,* January 7, 2018, http://www.courant.com/politics/capitol-watch/hc-pol-statute-of-limitations-sex-assault-20180104-story.html.

3. "Title VII, Civil Rights Act of 1964, as Amended," United States Department of Labor, accessed July 31, 2018, https://www.dol.gov/oasam/regs/statutes/2000e-16.htm.

4. Catalyst Information Center, *Why Diversity Matters,* July 2013, http://www.catalyst.org/system/files/why_diversity_matters_catalyst_0.pdf

5. Peter Economy, "Microsoft Just Announced Its Plan to End Secrecy around Sexual Harassment," *Inc.*, December 21, 2017, accessed July 31, 2018, https://www.inc.com/peter-economy/microsoft-just-announced-its-plan-to-end-secrecy-around-sexual-harassment.html.

6. Camila Domonoske, "Uber Will No Longer Force Sexual Assault Survivors into Arbitration or NDAs," NPR, May 15, 2018, https://www.google.com/url?rct=j&sa=t&url=https://www.npr.org/sections/thetwo-way/2018/05/15/611288966/uber-will-no-longer-force-sexual-assault-survivors-into-arbitration-or-.

7. Katy Steinmetz, "Facebook Just Published Its Sexual Harassment Policy. Here's Why," *Time*, December 8, 2017, http://time.com/5054763/facebook-sexual-harassment-policy-published/.

8. "De Blasio Signs Sweeping Workplace Anti-Sexual Harassment Laws," WCBS, May 10, 2018, https://wcbs880.radio.com/articles/de-blasio-signs-sweeping-workplace-anti-sexual-harassment-laws.

9. Jaime Herzlich, "New Law Requires All NY Employers to Have Policies to Prevent Sexual Harassment," *Newsday*, May 6, 2018, https://www.newsday.com/business/sexual-harassment-law-new-york-1.18379084.

10. Erica Morrison, "Nike Sees Executive Departures in Harassment Reckoning," NPR, May 15, 2018, https://www.npr.org/2018/05/15/610445057/nike-sees-executive-departures-in-harassment-reckoning?sc=tw; Julie, Creswell, Kevin Draper, and Rachel Abrams, "At Nike, Revolt Led by Women Leads to Exodus of Male Executives," *New York Times*, April 28, 2018, https://www.nytimes.com/2018/04/28/business/nike-women.html?emc=edit_nn_20180429.

11. Lulu Garcia-Navarro and Hiba Ahmad, "#MuteRKelly Co-Founder on the Moment, Her Movement and Its Momentum," NPR, May 6, 2018, accessed July 31, 2018,

https://www.npr.org/2018/05/06/608802024/-muterkelly-gathers-momentum.

12. "Time's Up Targets R. Kelly over Sexual Abuse Claims," CBS News, April 30, 2018, https://www.cbsnews.com/news/times-up-targets-r-kelly-over-sexual-abuse-claims/.

13. Nick Anderson, "University of Pennsylvania Revokes Honorary Degrees for Steve Wynn and Bill Cosby," *Washington Post*, February 1, 2018, accessed July 31, 2018, https://www.washingtonpost.com/news/grade-point/wp/2018/02/01/u-penn-revokes-honorary-degrees-for-steve-wynn-and-bill-cosby/?utm_term=.7ed84ed0abef.

# Chapter 10

1. Megyn Kelly, *Settle For More* (New York: HarperCollins, 2016), 211.

# About the Authors

## Brigitte Gawenda Kimichik, JD

Born and raised in Germany, Brigitte earned her Abitur in December 1980 from the Gymnasium Osdorf, in Hamburg, Germany, and came to the US thereafter to study. She earned her BBA in 1983 from the McCombs School of Business at the University of Texas at Austin, where she was a member of the Dean's List and the Golden Key Honor Society and graduated with honors after only two and a half years of study. She received her JD in 1986 from the Southern Methodist University Dedman School of Law in Dallas, Texas.

Over more than thirty years of experience as a commercial real-estate finance attorney, Brigitte was a partner at both Andrews Kurth LLP and Sheinfield, Maley, and Kay. From 1993 to 1997, Brigitte served on the board of the Wednesday's Child Benefit Corporation, and in 2012, she received the Most Powerful and Influential Women of Texas Award from the National Diversity Council.

Brigitte retired in 2015. She and her husband, David, live in Dallas, Texas. They are very proud of their two strong and intelligent daughters, Nicole and Samantha.

## JR (JoRayne) Tomlinson

JR Tomlinson earned her BBA in finance and investments from Texas Tech University in Lubbock, Texas. She earned her series 7, 63, and 22 licenses and began her career as a financial consultant with Merrill Lynch Pierce Fenner & Smith, Inc. Over a career spanning more than twenty-nine years, she has worked with Murray Properties, Public Storage, Jackson & Cooksey, Inc., and others. Her expertise in commercial real estate and the strategic alignment of corporate real estate has seen her manage numerous multimillion-dollar complex transactions for Fortune clients throughout North America. She has been honored to receive many awards as one of the best in her field, including a Dallas Power Broker Award from *D Magazine*, the US Green Council Building Award, and the Notable Women of Texas Award.

JR is currently a managing director with Newmark Knight Frank. She and her husband, Rob Hargis, live in Dallas, Texas.